Personality, Design and Marketing

T0313230

It is a marketing truism that products should be shaped around the preferences of customers, not designers, and that a design or advert that is effective with one personality type may not be effective with another. Since purchasing intent can be increased by providing products that appeal to particular types of customers, an understanding of the impact of personality on design will help maximise the effectiveness of design and advertising efforts.

This book reveals the extent to which design and advertising effectiveness can be improved through an understanding of the personalities of a range of stakeholders. While the impact of demographic factors (age, class, geographical location) is the object of considerable research, the impact of personality on production and preference aesthetics has been greatly overlooked. It is only by grouping together research conducted on diverse fields that a larger picture of the impact of personality on design production and preference aesthetics can be constructed.

Gloria Moss has brought together contributions from leading experts in academia and industry, including Professor Judi Harris, Dr Ceri Sims, Professor Paul Springer, Holly Buchanan and the late Bill Wylie. *Personality, Design and Marketing* will be of great interest to those who would like to see the effectiveness of design and marketing enhanced, whether it is those working in the area of design, or marketing or general management. It shows the extent to which preferences vary according to personality and the limitations of a one-size-fits-all approach to design.

Gloria Moss, the editor and author of several chapters in this volume, has a unique understanding of the impact of gender and nationality on graphic, product and web design and the steps organisations need to take to maximise design for end-users. She is a fellow of the Chartered Institute of Personnel and Development (CIPD) and currently holds the position of Professor of Marketing and Management at Buckinghamshire New University. Previously, Gloria has held senior positions in human resources and training and development at Courtaulds Acetate and Eurotunnel. Clients for consultancy on marketing and unconscious bias have included M&S, BT, Bounty, Ford, 02, Bayer and Allen and Overy.

Personality, Design and Marketing

Matching Design to Customer Personal
Preferences

Edited by Gloria Moss

Routledge
Taylor & Francis Group

LONDON AND NEW YORK

First published in paperback 2024

First published 2017
by Routledge
4 Park Square, Milton Park, Abingdon, Oxon OX14 4RN

and by Routledge
605 Third Avenue, New York, NY 10158

Routledge is an imprint of the Taylor & Francis Group, an informa business

British Library Cataloguing-in-Publication Data
A catalogue record for this book is available from the British Library

Library of Congress Cataloging-in-Publication Data
Names: Moss, Gloria, editor.
Title: Personality, design and marketing : matching design
    to customer personal preferences / edited by Gloria Moss.
Description: 1 Edition. | New York : Routledge, 2017. | Includes
    bibliographical references and index.
Identifiers: LCCN 2016037030 | ISBN 9780566087844 (hardback) |
    ISBN 9781315267821 (ebook)
Subjects: LCSH: Consumers—Psychology. | Marketing—Psychological
    aspects.
Classification: LCC HF5415.32 .P4697 2017 | DDC 658.8/342—dc23
LC record available at https://lccn.loc.gov/2016037030

ISBN: 978-0-566-08784-4 (hbk)
ISBN: 978-1-03-283794-9 (pbk)
ISBN: 978-1-315-26782-1 (ebk)

DOI: 10.4324/9781315267821

Typeset in Galliard
by Apex CoVantage, LLC

Contents

Figures

Tables

Contributors

Jim Blythe, PhD, has written 18 books and over 50 journal articles, and has contributed chapters to 8 other books. His work has been published in the *Journal of Marketing Management, Industrial Marketing Management, Journal of Business and Industrial Management, Marketing Intelligence and Planning* and many more. He is a former chair of the Academy of Marketing Special Interest Group for Qualitative Inquiry in Marketing and former editor of *Marketing Review*. He has taught overseas, written open-learning packs for international training organisations and has been a senior examiner for the Chartered Institute of Marketing.

Holly Buchanan is a popular speaker, consultant and the author of *Selling Financial Services to Women – What Men Need to Know and Even Women Will Be Surprised to Learn*. She is the co-author of *The Soccer Mom Myth*. Holly has spent the last decade studying and testing the differences between men and women – how they communicate, make decisions, and respond to sales and marketing campaigns. Her focus is the financial industry and further details can be found at www.SellingFinancialServicesToWomen.com and www.MarketAndSellToWomen.com.

Judi Harris, PhD, is a Professor and Pavey Family Chair in Educational Technology in the School of Education at the College of William & Mary in the US, where she coordinates the Curriculum and Educational Technology doctoral program. She teaches graduate courses in both educational technology and qualitative research design and methods, and assists doctoral students with dissertation work. Dr Harris's research and outreach work focus upon K-12 teacher learning and knowledge development, especially as they are reflected in instructional planning and the integration of digital tools and resources in classroom practice. During the past 37 years of her work with students and teachers using computing devices for learning and teaching, she has authored more than 240 research and pedagogical publications on curriculum-based applications of educational technologies. Judi's work is used by teachers, technology specialists and teacher educators internationally.

Gloria Moss, PhD, FCIPD, Professor of Management and Marketing at Buckinghamshire New University, combines a background as a training and development manager in Eurotunnel and Courtaulds with a career in academia and being the author of over 70 journal articles/conference papers as well as five books, including *Gender, Design and Marketing* (2009, Routledge), *Profiting from Diversity* (2010) and *Lessons on Profiting from Diversity* (2012) (both Palgrave Macmillan) and *Why Men Like Straight Lines and Women Like Polka Dots* (2014, Psyche). Her consultancy and research focus on the impact of nationality, gender and personality on leadership, teamwork, design and marketing, and she studies the challenges to organisations in achieving an 'outside-in' perspective so that they are able to deliver marketing and design solutions that have genuine appeal for target markets with varying demographic profiles. She led an industry-funded project on inclusive leadership and writes on this and other topics. She is a regular contributor to *Management Today*, *HR Magazine* and *Personnel Today*.

Ceri Sims, PhD, PGCertHE, CPsychol, MISCP, Senior Lecturer in Psychology at Buckinghamshire New University, was substantially involved in major developments of the Inclusive Leadership survey and assessment scales prepared as part of a funded study on inclusive leadership. As part of this, she was responsible for the operational management of the survey as well as for the statistical analyses and initial reporting on survey findings. Ceri is chartered by the British Psychological Society and is on its register of coaching psychologists. She was a research scientist for the Medical Research Council and has taught and researched at Durham, Newcastle, London and Middlesex universities. Her publications, mostly in peer-reviewed journals, range from developmental disorders in children to coaching students to overcome procrastination to multicultural perceptions of well-being. Her specialist areas for lecturing are occupational psychology, personality and individual differences, developmental psychology, coaching psychology and research methods. Ceri is also a Coaching Psychologist specialising in Positive Psychology Coaching.

Paul Springer PhD, MIoD, is a Professor of communications and associate dean of external development for the School of Arts & Digital Industries at the University of East London. He is author of *Pioneers of Digital* (2012), *Ads to Icons* (2008) (both Kogan Page) and *Saudi Advertising: Yesterday. Today. Tomorrow* (2013, Rumman KSA). Springer was the lead advisor for Saudi Arabia's first specialist college of communications and has worked on innovative media projects with WPP, Google Campus and the China Advertising Association, among others. He is the chair of the Research Committee for Edcom, the European Institute for Commercial Communications Education, and works with media firms on best practices in digital communications.

Bill Wylie (1944–2015) After training in drawing, painting and sculpture at the Glasgow School of Art and Edinburgh College of Art, Bill Wylie was awarded an MSc in art therapy at Queen Margaret University College, Edinburgh. Until 2010 he was head of art psychotherapy at HMP Grendon Therapeutic Community. He was a member of the Advisory Board of the Society for Indian Philosophy and Religion at Elon University. At the time of his death he was studying for a PhD in theology and religious studies at the University of Glasgow. His drawings and paintings have been exhibited both nationally and internationally and his art is in the public collections of Tayside Region and Leeds County.

Introduction – overview of the book

Gloria Moss

This book delves into the important but neglected topic concerning the way that personality impacts design and marketing creations and preferences. It looks at the extent to which personality shapes aspects of a design or piece of marketing and whether a positive response to design and marketing turns on a match between the personality of the creator and that of the observer? It then follows up on the implications for organisations, examining the way in which leadership and recruitment can help achieve an 'outside-in' perspective.

Why put the spotlight on this issue? There is a widespread recognition that business survival rests on shaping products or services around the 'unique and particular needs of the customer' (Hammer, 1995) and recognition of the importance of appealing to the customer's self-concept (Brock, 1965; Crozier and Greenhalgh, 1992; Karande et al., 1997; De Chernatony et al., 2004). This book explores the complex web of links that bind a product to its creator, on the one hand, and set up a pattern of liking with a beholder on the other. The particular focus is on the role that personality plays in shaping design and marketing *creations* and *references*.

The starting point for the book is personality and how it is approached by different commentators. The focus then shifts to several chapters investigating the links between personality and creations, then chapters investigating the links with personality and finally a chapter looking at organisational implications. In doing this, the book breaks new ground by taking design and marketing into the domains of art therapy and psychology and creating a base from which further research can evolve.

Personality

The opening chapter by Ceri Sims presents a comprehensive account of the major perspectives of personality developed by psychologists. The important contribution that dispositional traits play in understanding the variation in patterns of behaviour displayed by humans across various situations is discussed. Moreover, as well as providing a broad overview of a topic that has a rich history, the emphasis in this chapter is on emerging theories and recent developments in the field. One particular area that holds promise is the relatively modern field of positive psychology, where original humanistic theories meet modern scientific approaches, producing measures of individual differences in personality that serve to enhance positive behaviours and produce optimal human functioning. Developments in this field can offer insights into the kinds of traits and mindsets that allow creative designers to produce the most innovative and imaginative designs in their work.

The author introduces us to the multiple perspectives that allow personality to be discussed in a diversity of ways, an essential context to a field as extensive as human personality. The author aims to highlight the contrasts between these perspectives – for example by discussing the traits along which we all vary while also acknowledging the existence of elements of our character that make us all unique. Discussion includes also theories that emphasise the role of conscious thinking processes as well as those that describe the influence of the unconscious mind. It also explores evidence from neuropsychology and behavioural genetics and the role that life experience and culture can play in influencing people's identity and development across their lifespans. Appreciating the important contribution of theories ranging from the psychodynamic approaches of Freud and Jung to the more modern statistical and neuropsychological techniques of recent years can provide answers about individual differences in performance and motivation. Understanding these approaches can help in obtaining an understanding of the way in which the designer's personality can influence his or her visual creations and the way in which the personalities of the observers and customers will impact the kinds of designs that they are most attracted to.

Personality and creations

There are four chapters exploring the links between graphic expression and personality. The first by Gloria Moss takes a look at studies conducted several decades ago exploring the links between personality and graphic expression. These studies were conducted largely in the 1930s to 1960s, a period when the study received more attention than in later decades. Moss describes some of the landmark studies in this period, all of which show the strong connection binding personality to graphic expression. The first of these studies by Allport and Vernon (1933) evidenced the consistency present across different forms of graphic expression, something confirmed in experiments on handwriting and doodles by professor of psychology Wolff (1948). Wolff's experiments showed that four personality descriptions obtained separately in response to handwriting and doodles of different individuals could be successfully matched to single individuals in 70% of cases. The finding that personality is expressed in a consistent way across different forms of graphic expression makes it possible for findings in one area (e.g. drawings) to be extrapolated to that of another (e.g. paintings).

In what ways does personality manifest in graphic expression? Chapter 2 summarises the findings across numerous studies showing the way in which form and colour betoken personality traits. Of the most rigorous studies, by Waehner (1946) shows how size of graphics links to energy and anxiety levels; how curved shapes relate to introversion and creative impulses, and greater colour than form variety to energy, impetus and initiative. Burt's study (1968) moreover highlighted the extent to which Jung's so-called Intuitive types were more likely to avoid realistic images and more likely to use greater surface colour than the other types combined.

These studies offer a fascinating glimpse into the ways in which personality can influence the creative impulse, and given the hiatus that occurred in research after the flurry of activity in the 1930s through to the 1960s, we are fortunate to have three chapters written very recently. For the chapters by Wylie, Harris and Blythe amply demonstrate the extent to which the creator's personality is reflected in the created work, whether through the use made of space, colour, imagery or detail, and the way that an understanding of this can enrich a variety of environments.

Wylie's study (Chapter 3) involves an examination of the drawings of inmates of a therapeutic prison, showing how a study of these drawings can reveal much about the suitability of their creators to engage in group therapy. The close correlation that Wylie reports between the art therapist's assessment of suitability (based purely on an assessment of drawings) and that of an independent assessor demonstrates a high validity to the inference of personality from graphic expression. As Wylie writes, 'the self is externalised . . . [and] communicated through creativity.' A number of specific features are used as pointers in the analysis of the drawings. Where colour is concerned, a study assessing the impact of drawing topic on children's use of colour concluded that children tend to associate a negative emotion with dark colours, such as black or brown, while using yellow and orange to convey positive, happy feelings (Burkitt and Newell, 2005). Additionally, where size is concerned, it has been observed that this is used to convey the emotional significance of a topic, with appealing figures shown in exaggerated size and potentially threatening figures shown in reduced size (Thomas et al., 1989).

Moreover, temporal symbolism allows a picture to be read from left to right, from past to future, with the present centrally placed (Buck and Warren, 1995). It offers an X-ray image of the psychological state of the maker such that 'The proportion, perspective, and details in a drawing are general characteristics that can provide information about the functioning of an individual in the context of their expected level of functioning' (Buck and Warren, 1995, p. 25).

Blythe's study considered in Chapter 4 further considers the effect of the personality on graphic expression, examining this time the impact of personality on the work of advertising agency creatives. They were encouraged to describe the process of creating and interpreting brand personalities, to indicate which animal they most resembled and to say how this linked with their creative work. The creatives were also asked to bring samples of their 'best' work, a task they interpreted as an invitation to bring to samples of their favourite work. This response gave rise to discussion concerning the relationship between the individual and the piece of artwork or communication. The responses highlighted a connection between the personality of the creatives and that of the brand, with the brand reflecting the personality of its creator.

The implication for practitioners is that creatives will tend to produce work that reflects their own creative impulses, career aspirations, ethics and beliefs. In this way, creatives are likely to produce advertising that appeals primarily to themselves.

By implication, the traditional mechanistic model of communication is replaced, with a 'pool of meaning' model which highlights the interactive impact of personalities, whether those of the creatives, brand managers or consumers. In doing this, he moves beyond the traditional model of communications, in which 'the effect of personality [is] largely ignored', to an implied model in which part of the dialogue, and part of the development of branding, must involve the personalities of those who develop and deliver the message. A related consequence is that creatives tend to produce work which they find interesting and stimulating, rather than work which consumers will find interesting and stimulating. Coupled with the law of primacy (Lund, 1925), which states that earlier communications will take precedence over and colour the interpretation of later communications, it is possible to predict that creatives' preferences will take precedence over consumer preferences. One can see how the creatives' personalities can constitute a major obstacle to the achievement of the congruence with end-user preference advocated in the marketing literature (Moss, 2008). This tendency for creatives to produce work that mirrors their own personality could be entirely pernicious were it not for the fact that Blythe shows how clients tend to select agencies and creatives whose brand personalities are congruent with those of the promoted brand.

In Harris's Chapter 5 the focus moves to digital imagery and the way that this can reflect its creator's personality. Her study is similar to Wylie's insofar as it also examines the links between graphic expression and personality. She describes how 80 years of research have made it possible for artist characteristics such as intellectual acuity, developmental maturity, personality, values, attitudes, emotions, behaviour and culture of origin to be inferred from children's artistic works (LaVoy, 2001; Milne et al., 2005). She then describes empirical work in which she compared interview data regarding 9–10-year-old boys with the independent assessments of teachers who based their assessments entirely on an analysis of the boys' graphic expression. Levels of agreement were high, with 69% of teachers' comments in agreement with interview data. Only 21% of the teachers' comments contradicted interview data.

These results indicate the extent to which features of personality are mirrored in graphic expression and Harris underlines the importance of her findings by referring to the communicative equivalence of children's and adults' artwork (Silver, 1987; 1993) with similar results across age groups. She also describes the communicative equivalence of design and fine art creations, showing how scholars have drawn parallels between design and art for over 70 years.

In the final section of the book, the complex interplay of the personalities and genders of creatives and managers on the one hand and customers on the other is the subject of two chapters, one by Moss and one by Buchanan. The first of these chapters (Chapter 6) looks at preferences and the role that personality plays in a successful interplay between created product and observer preference. The second of these (Chapter 7) examines the way in which adjusting language on a website to the personality types of those visiting it can enhance visits to websites.

Moss's chapter investigates the role of personality in ensuring that consumers are satisfied with the visual images offered to them. Studies relating to preference are examined from the 1940s and brought together with findings relating to creations to determine whether preferences occur in a situation where the personalities of creator and observer are matched or in cases where they are different. The conclusion on examining eight studies is that preference appears more likely to occur where personalities are matched. In the specific area of advertising, a study by Hirsh et al. (2012) tested the extent to which the effectiveness of a persuasive message was increased when it was congruent with the recipient's personality profile. This hypothesis was tested by asking 324 subjects, all rated on the Big Five personality test, to rate the effectiveness of a variety of messages about a mobile phone. Each message had been created to respond to the particular motivations of each of the five types, and the results showed that there was an effect such that extravert subjects valued adverts focused on rewards and social attention; agreeable individuals valued adverts focused on communal goals and interpersonal harmony; conscientious individuals valued adverts focused on achievement, order and efficiency; neurotic individuals valued adverts presenting information about threats and uncertainty; and open individuals valued adverts that contained elements of creativity, innovation and intellectual stimulation.

The study, moreover, showed how an advertisement's rated effectiveness could increase with participants' scores on the targeted personality dimension, with responses on all personality types, bar neuroticism, correlating significantly with preferences for the matched advertisement. The authors conclude that manipulating the framing of an appeal to target the Big Five personality traits may provide a useful framework for marketers and that tailoring message is likely to be more effective than a one-size-fits-all campaign (Noar et al., 2007).

Where digital messages are concerned, a finding is reported on the fact that where emotional stability was concerned, a concept contrasted with neuroticism, emotionally stable personalities are less influenced by social anchors (e.g. ratings of products or services) than neurotic personality types (Arazy et al., 2015). Extensive information is also provided on the segmentation of the important 50-plus group of users by commentators (Sudbury and Simcock, 2011).

Buchanan's chapter likewise emphasises the importance of congruence between the personalities of the creator and observer, with the focus in this chapter being on the language used in websites. Buchanan shows clearly how the wording on the Internet can be adjusted to chime with the preferences of the personality types using the site. We see here how the author analysed the language used by those contributing to onsite reviews of a website specialising in women's clothing in order – following the homogeneity or congruity principle – to identify the style of language that should be used on the website. The author read hundreds of customer reviews and, following analysis, judged that the preferred communication style was, in Jungian terms, the Sensing, Feeling and Perceiving type (SFP). All these traits are in fact opposite in type to that of the owner/copywriter and so, in order to satisfy the preferences of the end-users, the author changed the voice of the website and emails from the Intuitive, Thinking and Judgement type (NTJ) to the Sensing, Feeling and Perceiving type (SFP).

In an A/B email test, one version was written in the old style (NTJ) and one version was written in the new style (SFP), and the new style (SFP) achieved a 27% higher click-through rate. The client was convinced that the new copy was effective, clearly recognised the benefits of diversity and made changes throughout the site.

Springer's chapter looks, like Buchanan's, at personality and language and presents two case studies of digital communities gathered around pop music artists. The first is a digital community gathered around the band One Direction that communicates to the band and to each other on social media sites. The second is the community of followers that participates with messages on the singer Ellie Goulding's website. In the second case, visitors consist of opted-in core followers and co-opted 'seeded followers', both of whom are targeted to the website by data analysts and marketing specialists employed by the artist's record label.

Springer appraises the correlation between the personality of visitors and the personality of the websites themselves, thereby establishing whether the homogeneity principle is operating here with similarity in personality type between visitor and website. He does this by reviewing the nature of social media participation as evidenced through an examination of fans' tweets and posted messages, posted to each other and to the artists, examining patterns of address, tone, message style and subject matter. This study leads him to conclude that message-posters tend to reinforce the personal characteristics of the artists that they follow as well as of the participants on artists' web spaces. Springer then applies the findings to recent neurosocial and marketing psychology, proposing factors that drive similar personality types to become active messengers in like-minded communities.

In the final chapter of the book, Moss outlines the organisational steps needed to achieving a match between the personality of the creator (as reflected in the commercial visual image) and that of the consumer. These steps involve grappling with the homogeneity principle that can lead organisations to recruit people like themselves (Lewis, 2006), employing creatives whose values match those of senior staff rather than those of the purchaser or end user. Such a mismatch between internal organisational values and external customer values can unfortunately prevent organisations from achieving the congruence with customer preferences advocated in the marketing literature. Only a concerted attempt to organisational internal stakeholders on the value of alternative ways of seeing may enable an organisation to overcome these difficulties. Otherwise, we can find organisational actors making choices that conflict with target customer preferences, an outcome that can be avoided by ensuring that HR policies and strategies (recruitment and promotion) and marketing decisions (selection of branding and designs) emphasise the need to prioritise the needs of external rather than internal stakeholders.

Of course, doing this is not easy. The path to success is strewn with obstacles, many of which have been highlighted in earlier work (Moss et al., 2008). These factors include management and leadership constructs that favour the appointment/promotion of personalities and genders that may be at odds with the personalities and genders of the target constituency, leading in turn to the appointment and promotion of creatives whose personalities and genders are at variance with those of the target constituency. Underlying these points is the assumption, amply demonstrated in the chapters by Harris, Wylie, Blythe and Buchanan, that creative output is highly correlated with personality type and gender. In an era of intensifying competition, delivering products that appeal to specific customer segments is a high priority (Wesson and Figueiredo, 2001). Given the importance of the principle of congruence and, within this, the role of *product preference* in increasing attention span, the ability to understand and remove obstacles to the achievement of congruence and *product preference* must be a key priority.

Of course, to understand the roots of a problem is not to find complete solutions. Further work could usefully focus on developing the models discussed in this volume so that a more detailed picture is gained of the complex interplay between personality and gender necessary to create the congruence between end user and product advocated in the marketing literature. Future work could also usefully examine and evaluate methods for overcoming a perceived lack of congruence between staff and customer segmentation variables. These methods might include training for HR and marketing personnel on the impact of segmentation variables (personality and gender) on production and preference aesthetics, as well as ways of encouraging recruitment and promotion processes that are in line with the preferences of external rather than simply internal customers.

I would like finally to thank my fellow contributors for participating in this special edition. They are all busy, professional people and I appreciate this response to requests for revisions from myself or reviewers, and meeting the tight deadlines required of this collection.

References

Allport, G. W. and Vernon, P. E. (1933). *Studies in Expressive Movement*. New York: Macmillan.

Arazy, O., Nov, O. and Kumar, N. (2015). Personalityzation: UI personalization, theoretical grounding in HCI and design research. *AIS Transactions on Human-Computer Interaction (AIS THCI)*, 7(2), pp. 43–69.

Brock, T. C. (1965). Communicator-recipient similarity and decision change. *Journal of Personality and Social Psychology*, 1, pp. 650–654.

Buck, J. N. and Warren, W. L. (1995). House-Tree-Person. Projective Drawing Technique: Manual and Interpretive Guide. Los Angeles Western Psychological Services.

Burkitt, E. and Newell, T. (2005). Effects of human figure on children's use of colour to depict sadness and happiness. *International Journal of Art Therapy*, 10(1), pp. 15–22.

Burt, R. B. (1968). *An Exploratory Study of Personality Manifestations in Paintings*. Doctoral dissertation, Duke University (Dissertation Abstracts International 29, 1493–B Order number 68–14, 298).

Crozier, W. and Greenhalgh, P. (1992). The empathy principle: Towards a model for the psychology of art. *Journal for the Theory of Social Behaviour*, 22, pp. 63–79.

De Chernatony, L., Drury, S. and Segal-Horn, S. (2004). Identifying and sustaining services brands values. *Journal of Marketing Communications*, 10, pp. 73–94.

Hammer, M. (1995). *Reengineering the Corporation*. London: Nicholas Brealey.

Hirsh, J. B., Kang, S. K. and Bodenhausen, G. V. (2012). Personalized persuasion tailoring persuasive appeals to recipients' personality traits. *Psychological Science*, 23(6), pp. 578–581.

Karande, K., Zinkhan, G. M. and Lum, A. B. (1997). Brand Personality and Self Concept: A Replication and Extension. *American Marketing Association, Summer Conference*, pp. 165–171.

LaVoy, D.J. (2001). Trust and reliability. *Public Management*, 30(30), p. 8.

LaVoy, S. K., Pedersen, W. C., Reitz, J. M., Brauch, A. A., Luxenberg, T. M. and Nofsinger, C. C. (2001). Children's drawings: A cross-cultural analysis from Japan and the United States. *School Psychology International*, 22(1), pp. 53–63.

Lewis, C. (2006). Is the test relevant? *Times*, Career section, 30 November, p. 8.

Lund, F. H. (1925). The psychology of belief, the law of primacy in persuasion. *Journal of Abnormal and Social Psychology*, 20, pp. 183–191.

Milne, L. C., Greenway, P. and Best, F. (2005). Children's behaviour and their graphic representation of parents and self. *Arts in Psychotherapy*, 32(2), pp. 107–119.

Moss, G., Gunn, R. and Kubacki, K. (2008). Angling for beauty: Commercial implications of an interactive aesthetic for web design. *International Journal of Consumer Studies*, 30, pp. 1–14.

Moss, G., Gunn, R.W. and Kubacki, K. (2008). Gender and web design: The implications of the mirroring principle for the services branding model. *Journal of Marketing Communications*, 14(1), pp. 37–57.

Noar, S. M., Benac, C. N. and Harris, M. S. (2007). Does tailoring matter? Meta-analytic review of tailored print health behaviour change interventions. *Psychological Bulletin*, 133, pp. 673–693.

Silver, R. A. (1987). Sex differences in the emotional content of drawings. *Art Therapy*, 4(2), pp. 67–77.

Silver, R. A. (1992). Gender differences in drawings: A study of self-images, autonomous subjects, and relationships. *Art Therapy*, 9(2), pp. 85–92.

Silver, R. A. (1993). Age and gender differences expressed through drawings: A study of attitudes toward self and others. *Art Therapy*, 10(3), pp. 159–168.

Sudbury, L. and Simcock, P. (2011). Bargain Hunting Belongers and Positive Pioneers: Key Silver Market Segments in the UK. In: *The Silver Market Phenomenon: Marketing and Innovation in the Aging Society*. Edited by: F. Kohlbacher and C. Herstatt. pp. 195–202. London: Springer.

Thomas, G. V., Chaigne, E. and Fox, T. J. (1989). Children's drawings of topics differing in significance: Effects on size of drawing. *British Journal of Developmental Psychology*, 7, pp. 321–331.

Waehner, T. S. (1946). Interpretations of spontaneous drawings and paintings. *Genetic Psychology Monograph*, 33, pp. 3–70.

Wesson, T. and De Figueiredo, J. N. (2001). The importance of focus to market entrants: A study of microbrewery performance. *Journal of Business Venturing*, 16, pp. 377–403.

Wolff, W. (1948). *Diagrams of the Unconscious*. New York: Grune and Stratton.

Chapter 1

The psychology of personality

Ceri Sims

> *We cannot choose between the approaches to personality based on which one is right. A better criterion for evaluating a psychological approach is this: Does it offer a way to seek an answer to a question you feel is worthwhile? . . . Which do you need or want to know about? The answer to this question tells you which approach to use.*
>
> (Funder, 2010, p. 743)

Personality psychologists are concerned with the consistent patterns of thoughts, feelings and behaviours that differentiate people from each other. Personality *traits* form the conceptual bedrock of personality psychology. Without traits, people would be inconsistent and unpredictable. We would have no means of deciding whom to choose as our best friends, work alliances or business leaders because people would be behaving randomly. Some differential psychologists also call themselves trait theorists. Adopting the position of a trait theorist usually goes beyond the assumption that people have enduring dispositions that predict their behavioural patterns. It also assumes that there are a limited and small set of core traits that can be measured using psychometric methods involving the construction and validation of questionnaires and personality tests. The continuing appeal of this approach is threefold; first, it has generated a wealth of research; second, it has expanded our conceptualisation about the personality characteristics that describe people throughout the world; third, it enables quantifiable measurement of personality traits that can be used to predict various important facets of human functioning. These measurements include happiness, marital success, job performance and longevity.

Explanations of human personality have a long tradition of theorising that stands outside the mainstream of trait approaches. Furthermore, modern perspectives, such as positive psychology, recent conceptual leaps in cognitive psychology and the emergence of modern psychodynamic viewpoints, are offering alternative ways of conceptualising and measuring people's characteristics and each has a different focus. In fact, having a variety of theoretical perspectives is valuable for understanding something as vital to humanity as personality. Not surprisingly, we still await the discovery of that single grand theory that can tell us everything we need to know about how a person's feelings, thoughts, actions, interactions, motives and preferences make up his or her complete personality. Therefore, while each approach has its merits and limitations, it is quite reasonable to 'sit on the fence' and not feel any obligation to choose one perspective as being the right one. Indeed, in this chapter, the point being made is that it is advisable to consider that there may be both conscious and unconscious routes to personality development; that examining one's motivation for growth and development need not contradict those views that focus on people's conflicts within the psyche; and that measuring one's traits as behavioural patterns does not negate the importance of exploring and understanding both the cognitive processes and neurological activities underlying those patterns. Moreover, just because many theorists and researchers of differential psychology concentrate on knowing more about those important human traits that appear to be universal, this does not undermine the significance of examining how the broader culture and experience can account for wide inter-individual differences. Major life experiences and deliberate self-development can promote intra-individual changes in people's personality traits at different phases across their lives. Thus, each of the different perspectives has something useful and important to offer in aspiring towards a complete picture of the multifaceted psychological constituents that make people different from each other and that define who they are as unique individuals.

The first section in this chapter compares the viewpoint that traits are an inclusive set of dispositions shared by all people against a different viewpoint that an individual's underlying traits are exclusive to only that particular person. The mainstream trait approach largely adopts the former perspective, and this is compared to the view of personality as being essentially idiosyncratic rather than comparable across every one of us. In the second section, the comparison is made between psychodynamic perspectives (that tend to focus on unresolved early life experiences and the unconscious mind) and cognitive theories (that examine the largely consciously accessible thinking habits that make people who they are). The third section addresses the issue of the role of biology versus experience on personality, examining evidence of inherited temperamental differences between individuals and discussing how experience and nature interact in the development of personality across the lifespan. The fourth section of the chapter discusses a set of theories and research about personality that can be subsumed under the umbrella of positive psychology. Historically, personality theorists have often also been clinicians with an interest in personality pathology. Positive psychology strays from this tradition by considering the overarching driving force of human nature as leaning towards healthy personality development and flourishing.

Are there universal personality traits or are people unique?

Most definitions of the term 'traits' mention that they are consistent and stable patterns of thoughts, feelings and behaviours that differentiate people from each other. Therefore it is safe to say that we can think of the collection of individual traits that one possesses as being the linchpin of one's personality. The major difference between different factions of personality researchers and theorists is whether to identify a set of universal traits against which people can be compared or whether to focus on a person's own underlying personality traits as particular to his or her own unique psychological make-up. Psychologists who call themselves trait theorists are usually interested in the former, identifying dispositions that apply to everyone to some extent. This is also known as the *nomothetic* approach to measuring personality. The *idiographic* approach, by contrast, emphasises the uniqueness of individual features as being most important. Those who use idiographic methods regard the underlying traits of individuals as being specific to their own set of personal experiences, values and attitudes. On the whole, it is humanistic, psychodynamic and social-cognitive researchers who choose this latter approach.

Trait theorists are concerned with ways of measuring a person's underlying dispositions or traits or are interested in assessing differences in a set of core trait dimensions in order to predict individual differences in a variety of outcomes. Research has been extensive in this regard, examining the relationship between personality traits and various measures of life choices, social roles, achievement levels and areas of satisfaction, ranging very widely from examples such as personality influences on healthy lifestyles (e.g. Hampson et al., 2006; Ozer and Benet-Martinez, 2006) and personality characteristics in the use of online social networking sites (Correa, Hinsley and De Zuniga, 2010) to examining the traits of Mount Everest climbers (Egan and Stelmack, 2003). The assumption is that we can identify a small set of universally important traits that can be measured in everyone when making predictions about outcomes. This perspective also adopts particular methods of investigation and measurement. One such method has been the lexical approach, which assumes that the trait terms appearing frequently in natural language across cultures are just those terms that are candidates for a universal taxonomy of personality traits. For example groundbreaking research in the 1930s by Allport and Odbert (1936) discovered 17,953 trait terms in the English dictionary, from which 4,500 stable traits were identified, which included adjectives such as *aggressive, honest* and *intelligent*. Trait theorists have proposed different organisational frameworks of traits. Allport identified three levels of traits: the cardinal trait (one that dominates), central traits (those that shape most of behaviour) and secondary traits (traits specific to particular circumstances). Interestingly while it was Allport's work that paved the way for the trait approach to identify a small set of the most significant dispositions present in all people, it was also Allport who proposed that most traits refer to relatively unique dispositions that are based on one's own particular life experiences. Therefore, he advocated using an idiographic approach.

Trait theorists since Allport have been drawn to nomothetic methods of investigation. Using a plethora of investigative material through methods of observation, self-report and laboratory tests, the British psychologist Raymond Cattell (1943) recognised many similarities among Allport and Odbert's trait terms and clustered these traits together into a much smaller number of trait clusters, using a statistical technique known as factor analysis. Factor analysis is an efficient way of identifying groups of trait terms that co-vary with each other (go together) and that do not co-vary with other items. Eventually, what starts as a large number of trait adjectives gets reduced right down to a much smaller set of essential core dispositions that are regarded as the main dimensions along which all people vary. Cattell refined his traits down to 16 personality factors (Cattell, Eber and Tatsuoka, 1970). Cattell also distinguished between different trait levels, including surface and source (underlying) traits, as well as further sub-categories of source traits, such as dynamic (motivational) traits and temperament traits.

Another key trait theorist is Hans Eysenck, who started off with his own theory of the biological significance of core temperaments before devising his personality inventory and using factor analytic methods of data reduction (Eysenck, 1967). Eysenck argued that *extraversion/ introversion (E)* and *emotional stability/instability (N)* were the main dimensions along which all people varied. He subsequently added the trait of *psychoticism (P)* to his theory, although his E and N factors have gained much more supportive evidence than his P factor.

By far the most popular support has been for the five-factor theory of Paul Costa and Robert McCrae (1995). An explosion of evidence has accumulated on measures of what has become known as their Big Five factors, these being *openness to experience, conscientiousness, extraversion, agreeableness* and *neuroticism (emotional stability)*. Openness reflects the degree of intellectual curiosity, creativity and preference for novelty and variety a person has. Conscientiousness reflects a tendency to be organised and dependable and a preference for planned rather than spontaneous behaviour. Extraversion is characterised as showing qualities such as being energetic, assertive and sociable as opposed to choosing to keep one's own company and a preference for quiet surroundings (introverted). Agreeableness is a tendency to be compassionate and cooperative rather than suspicious and antagonistic towards others. Finally, neuroticism is the predilection for experiencing anxiety, anger or depression. A person with low scores on this dimension is regarded as emotionally stable and not vulnerable to experiencing negative emotional reactions.

This model has been widely replicated and is shown to be remarkably robust across many large samples (Goldberg, 1990). While this chapter cannot do justice to the vast amount of research on life outcomes predicted from the Big Five, some of the key findings that have been replicated are that high conscientiousness and low neuroticism (high emotional stability) are predictive of good student grades (Chamorro-Premuzic and Furnham, 2003; Richardson, Abraham and Bond, 2012) and lower procrastination (Watson, 2001); leadership effectiveness in business is predicted by high extraversion, high openness and low neuroticism (Silverthorne, 2001); happiness is best predicted by high extraversion and low neuroticism (Cheng and Furnham, 2003); aggression towards others is predicted mostly by neuroticism (Hellmuth and McNulty, 2008), whereas neuroticism accompanied by high agreeableness reduces the frequency of angry outbursts (Barlett and Anderson, 2012). Moreover, a combination of high neuroticism, high extraversion and low conscientiousness increases the chances of risky and addictive behaviours, such as heavy alcohol consumption (Grano, Virtanen, Vahtera, Elovainio and Kivimaki, 2004); and multiple risky sexual behaviours can be predicted from low agreeableness, low openness and high extraversion (Miller et al., 2004). Finally, a recent study shows that while high extraversion predicts assertive communication, it is high levels of traits of agreeableness and openness that are linked with having high levels of active and empathic listening (Sims, 2016), a finding that suggests that while an extravert might ask questions and seek social encounters, people with 'agreeable' and 'open' traits may be superior conversationalists when it comes to engaging with and considering other people's views and opinions.

One of the major controversies surrounding the five-factor model is whether it provides a comprehensive account of personality (Block, 1995). While there is a general consensus that the Big Five are the most relevant dimensions of personality, those who offer a cautionary position tend to consider five factors as offering too limited a scope to provide a complete account of all human characteristics. Dan McAdams (1992) has made the strong case that the five-factor model comprises a 'psychology of the stranger' – that is the five factors describe what one might want to know if one knew nothing else about a person. These criticisms to trait approaches focus on the 'rough and ready' classification of personality measured through personality inventories. Idiographic methods are recommended when one wants to gain a deeper and more thorough portrait of the desires, goals and personal identities of particular individuals.

In spite of the strong evidence of the predictive validity of the Big Five, these core traits are not perfect predictors of either current behaviour or future life outcomes. Wide variations in experience, situational complexities and developmental influences will interact with basic dispositions leading to a vast number of different possible outcomes. Therefore, while personality profiles can be useful predictors, they should not be regarded as fortune tellers.

Cross-cultural studies have also indicated that those dispositions regarded as important by researchers in American society may not be appropriate for measuring personality in other parts of the world. Sagiv and Roccas (2000) have investigated the role of cultural values in trait expression, with extraversion and openness being more readily endorsed in Western cultures, and cooperation and tradition being more valued in non-Western cultures. Some researchers have developed different factors using the natural language of their own countries. For example in China and South Africa, researchers have developed their own measures of personality as well as identifying culture-specific personality traits (Cheung, van de Vijver and Leong, 2011).

The idiographic position involves a very different approach. It assumes that people have features of personality that are personal to themselves and that each individual has his or her own life history that brings about a unique and idiosyncratic way of thinking, feeling and being. Those who adopt an idiographic approach use methods such as focus groups, interviews or in-depth case studies. These investigative approaches can yield rich and meaningful information about individuals that psychometric scales are unable to uncover. (Runyan, 1983, offers a thorough discussion of the goals and methods of the idiographic method.) One of the major criticisms of such methods is their high level of subjective interpretation and their inability to yield findings that meet the criteria of scientific validity. Humanistic, psychodynamic and social-cognitive theorists have leaned towards a focus on the unique experiences of individuals. The humanistic approach is discussed later in the section on developing a flourishing personality (positive psychology). Probably the most renowned and notorious personality psychologist, Sigmund Freud, used a clinical interview method in developing his psychoanalytic theory of personality. His approach was to write up his notes at the end of the day rather than during therapeutic sessions to allow his patients to express their thoughts and feelings freely and naturally. The cognitive theorist George Kelly developed an idiographic method known as the Role Repertory Test (RRT), which is still used today in both clinical and occupational contexts. Essentially, the RRT was designed to permit individuals to openly disclose information about themselves and other people known to them using their own language, allowing the investigator or therapist to understand an individual's personal constructs (Kelly, 2003). Psychodynamic and cognitive approaches to personality will be compared and discussed further in the next section.

What psychological factors underpin personality: unconscious conflicts or conscious patterns of thinking?

Some differential psychologists simply regard traits as descriptive summaries of personality attributes, without making any assumptions about internal causal properties. However, other theorists of various traditions have offered explanations, considering particular mental phenomena to be at the heart of their account of personality. In this section, the psychodynamic and cognitive schools will be compared, as they provide quite different explanatory theories. The different traditions of these two perspectives do share one thing in common – namely that personality is regarded as portraying the person that individuals become once mental activities play havoc with and influence emotional reactions. Beyond that, however, the two approaches are quite different. On the one hand, the psychodynamic approach concentrates on the unconscious and hidden elements of the mind, whereas cognitive theorists largely focus on understanding how conscious thought processes influence our ways of responding and interacting with the world. Furthermore, in managing dysfunctional personalities, the psychodynamic school generally believes that lengthy periods of psycho-analysis are required for recovery, whereas cognitive psychologists usually advocate shorter periods of cognitive-behavioural therapy.

Freud proposed that personalities have three components: the id, the ego and the super-ego (Freud, 1927). The id is the place in the mind that energises impulses towards survival, sex and aggression, and is otherwise known as the 'pleasure principle'. The ego operates according to the 'reality principle', working in such a way that the impulses of the id are managed to accommodate the socially appropriate demands of the real world. The super-ego's role is also to manage the expression of desires, but so that they meet moral standards. For example a person would feel guilty if he or she expressed desires that went against the norms of society. Freud's theory was groundbreaking and led to many followers. However, the psychodynamic theorists who extended his theory also questioned some of his central arguments, such that some of Freud's original ideas, particularly his emphasis on psycho-sexual determinism, are now almost universally considered to be out of date.

The neo-Freudians continued to emphasise the significance of unconscious motives, con-flicts existing within the psyche and the role of early experiences in shaping personality. Alfred Adler's 'individual psychology' (1924) moved away from Freudian libidinous and aggressive instincts to a focus on strivings for superiority and the notion of the inferior-ity complex. The object relations school, for which Donald Winnicott and Melanie Klein are renowned (Grotstein, 1991), regards interpersonal relationships to be the central drive for personality, with 'objects' being internalised representations of significant others from early relationships, particularly the mother; Karen Horney's 'relational approach' focused on conflicts as unresolved interpersonal issues and responses to cultural expectations of masculinity and femininity. Horney debunked Freud's idea that females experience 'penis envy' and developed a theory devoid of such sexual prejudices. A collective volume of her work has been published (Horney, 2000). Erik Erikson examined stages of development as Freud did, but his stages were psychosocial rather than psychosexual and his focus was more on the ego (reality principle) rather than on the fully unconscious id (pleasure principle). In an atypical psychodynamic fashion, Erikson's stages spanned the complete lifespan and, after he died, his wife Joan developed a final ninth stage for people living into their nineties and beyond (Erikson and Erikson, 1998). Erikson's theory dealt with conflicts such as identity development in adolescence as well as wisdom and a sense of accomplishment versus despair in older adulthood. Although this theory still emphasises intra-psychic conflicts underlying one's personality, the lifespan approach is consistent with the view that environmental fac-tors interact with personal factors at different phases across the entire life. In this regard, Erikson's is a theory that challenges core trait theories of personality, where the focus is mostly on biological maturation and the relatively unchanging nature of one's personality beyond middle age.

One psychodynamic concept that continues to have substantial research appeal is that of 'defence mechanisms'. Freud discussed how the ego employs unconscious defences, such as repression (the burying of a painful thought from one's awareness), to protect the id, which is suffering anxiety originating from unresolved conflicts fixated during childhood stages of development. Many of Freud's patients revealed the defences they were using because the anxieties leaked out in specific ways, such as through symptoms of illness, recurrent dreams and slips of the tongue. In 1936, Freud's daughter, Anna, researched defence mechanisms in more depth, regarding them as responses to social stresses. Recently a team of American researchers, led by the psychiatrist George Vaillant, has focused on adaptive defences that are predictive of job and relationship successes. Their focus is on mature defences, such as intellectualisation, humour and altruism. Adults who adopt mature defences to cope with life's adversities are healthier in old age compared to those people who persist with using immature ones (Malone et al., 2013).

One of the biggest criticisms of psychodynamic approaches is that Freudian concepts can be dogmatic and lacking in methodology. This criticism is mostly targeted against the writings of Freud himself. To illustrate, Freud (1960, cited in Reason, 2000) was discussing a holiday trip where he met a young man who misquoted the Latin phrase 'Exoriare aliquis nostris ex ossibus ultor,' which translates to 'Let someone arise as an avenger from my bones,' but the young man misquoted and instead suppressed the word 'aliquis' (someone). Using psychoanalytic techniques of free word association, the word became associated with the German for 'relics' and then to 'liquids' and then to a series of different saints, then through further associations to the word 'blood', leading to the inference that the man was making a Freudian slip because he feared that a woman whom he had intercourse with had missed a menstruation cycle. The interpretation of this, according to Freud, was that he was fearful of becoming a father!

It is lengthy examples of obscure associations such as these that enable us to appreciate how one of the earliest cognitive theorists, George Kelly, came to completely dismiss Freud's theory as 'nonsense'. Kelly made the claim that personality is the outcome of the personal constructs that people form, and from this he went on to develop a formal theory to support his position (Kelly, 2003). Kelly argued that it is the habitual ways that people go about interpreting and predicting the events in their lives that determine how they are likely to behave. For example if we usually perceive other people as trustworthy and friendly, then we are more likely to approach others for advice and support. On the other hand, if we regard people as hostile and antagonistic, we are more likely to deal with troubles alone and avoid others. Quite unlike Freud, Kelly perceived people as rational beings, adapting to the challenges of their world and essentially free in the choices they make. Decisions were often conscious ones according to Kelly, although he used the term 'preverbal' to acknowledge mental constructs that can occur outside of awareness.

Although cognitive approaches are often considered to be fundamentally different to psychodynamic ones, one key cognitive theorist, Albert Ellis, is in fact a cognitive therapist who was originally influenced by prominent neo-Freudian therapists, such as Adler, Horney and Fromm, in developing his own model. His own approach deviated from the others because of his core belief that people's irrational thoughts were responsible for their self-defeating emotional and behavioural patterns. Ellis's (2004) rational-emotive therapy works on the principle that emotional responses (anger, fear, depression) are a consequence of holding particular beliefs about events, and that changing these unhelpful thinking habits requires cognitively reappraising a situation in a more rational and constructive manner. A shy individual is likely to have many memories and feelings associated with experiences of rejection and being treated disrespectfully by others, such that his or her perceptual system is on high alert, or primed to react with withdrawal at the slightest indication of unfriendliness by another. For this person to change to a more socially outgoing person would involve learning to undo those habitual thinking patterns. One way would be to adopt a more rational view of, say, considering that if a person is not being very friendly then there can be many reasons for it – for example perhaps the person is shy or is having a bad day. Although cognitive theories appreciate that thinking habits can be difficult to break, cognitive therapy lasts for shorter periods than psychoanalyses, where sessions can continue for years. This is because cognitive approaches acknowledge that people are free to choose more rational and helpful patterns of construing the world without the need to delve into a person's early life history to remedy hidden and long-established childhood conflicts.

In spite of the term 'neo-Freudian', some psychodynamic perspectives are far removed from Freudian determinism. Take Erich Fromm as an example. Fromm saw humans as having existential needs that transcend animal needs and lead to anxieties that can be resolved only through the spontaneous activity of the integrated personality. Fromm asserted that 'Man's main task in life is to give birth to himself, to become what he potentially is. The most important product of his effort is his own personality' (Fromm, 1947, p. 237). For this reason Fromm is sometimes cited as being probably the first humanistic psychologist.

Another psychodynamic theorist who has contributed in many ways to investigating and understanding personality is Carl Jung. He introduced the term 'collective unconscious', which contains universal memories of the common human past that Jung called 'archetypes'. Archetypes exist in dreams as well as in art, literature and religion across cultures (Jung, 1963). Although Jung is often remembered for his religious and esoteric ideas, he was the first major theorist to recognise the key significance of extraversion and introversion as core 'attitudes' of personality. From this he developed a typology model (Jung, 1923), whereby people were regarded as either introverted or extraverted (a somewhat different perspective to the common dimensional view of extraversion that is accepted by trait approaches). Jung also identified four psychic functions: two rational functions requiring acts of judging (Thinking T and Feeling F) and two functions for perceiving immediate experiences (Sensation S and Intuition I). His theory continues to have enormous impact in the assessment of personality types in the workplace as it underpins one of the most widely used personality measurements in organisations today: the Myers-Briggs Type Indicator (MBTI: Myers, McCaulley and Most, 1985). The MBTI measures personality type using a self-report inventory that identifies a total of 16 typologies based on all combinations of attitude type (Extravert or Introvert), decision-making type (T or F), perception type (S and I) and an additional type added by Katherine Briggs and her daughter Isabel Myers called lifestyle type (either a preference for the Judging function [J] or a preference for the Perceiving function [P]). So for example an ENTJ type is someone who is extraverted and intuitive, uses reasoning to make decisions and shows a general preference for making judgements over relying on immediate perceptions.

What roles do nature and nurture play in the development of a stable personality?

By now it should be clear that personality traits are considered to be relatively enduring aspects of a person. Trait theorists (McCrae and Costa, 2008) often consider the stability of traits as being a reflection of inborn and biological factors, enabling different people to be predisposed to develop particular traits more strongly than others. However, the stability assumption of personality is not always accepted without contention. While completely erratic behaviour undermines the concept of personality altogether, some researchers have maintained that personality predictability is limited to how a person is likely to behave in a particular situation. This rather different emphasis on defining personality is illustrated by Walter Mischel's cognitive-affective theory of personality (Mischel and Shoda, 1995).

Mischel's theory focuses on how traits and situations interact to predict how a person will act during a particular experience. Mischel and Shoda (1995) believe that expectancies, subjective perceptions, values, goals, personal standards and emotions are important in shaping personality. Thus a person with an aggressive personality may have high expectations for success accompanied by the belief that aggressive behaviour is permissible to achieve a goal. For the person with an aggressive personality, if the situation creates goal-frustration then an aggressive outburst is likely to occur. However, if the situation allows the person to progress towards a successful goal without obstacles, then the same person is more likely to remain calm. Since Mischel made his 'situationist' critique of early trait approaches, further interest in the interactions between traits and environments has developed. However, while the manifestation of certain behaviours within individuals will vary according to the cues of the situation (e.g. a person with high levels of extraversion is more likely to express sociable behaviours in large groups than in small groups), the core traits of the five-factor model still show a reasonable degree of consistency across a variety of situations (Fleeson, 2001).

A central argument of the trait approach is that the essential traits within the personality taxonomy can be used to classify people's personalities throughout the world. Underlying this assumption is the view that the universality of such traits is a natural product of evolution, such that over history these traits have been selected for the survival of the species (Buss and Greiling, 1999). Integral to the evolutionary argument is that the reason why we have opposite poles on these traits is that both extremes have advantages for survival. So for example high versus low agreeableness is accounted for by differences between people in their proclivity to be cooperative versus being selfish over gaining limited resources. Being cooperative with other people within the same group ensures that everyone gets a slice of the pie. Selfish individuals would be undesirable and persecuted by intolerant group members. On the other hand, when resources are very scarce, people who do not fight their own corner starve, so evolution has also favoured some degree of low agreeableness for survival. The same argument applies to the other core traits: neuroticism relates to the gains from being sensitive to social dangers over the cost of emotional anxieties and stress; extraversion is a survival trait for risk-taking, whereas introverts reap the survival benefits of long-term family stability; conscientiousness reflects the cost-benefit survival of immediate rewards over delayed gratification; openness brings invaluable creative benefits, but there is also a relationship between psychosis and openness in extremely creative individuals, implying that there are advantages to adopting more rigid patterns of thinking (Nettle, 2006).

Some key personality theorists, notably Eysenck (1967), set out to explain individual differences in biological terms. For example he argued that extraversion was a result of physiological differences in a part of the brain known as the reticulo-cortical region, an area controlling patterns of cortical arousal to incoming stimuli. He argued that introverts have higher levels of cortical arousal than extraverts, who seek external stimulation to compensate for having lower levels. This would explain why introverted people prefer quiet environments whereas extraverts prefer noise and loud parties.

One field of research that attempts to determine the degree to which personality differences are caused by genetic and environmental differences is the area known as behavioural genetics. The goal of this field for personality is to decipher the proportion of individual differences in particular traits within the human population that are heritable (accounted for by genetic variance) and to establish how genetic and environmental variations influence each other. Much behavioural genetic research on personality uses twin studies. If we accept that non-identical (fraternal) twins share about half of their genes in the same way that siblings do and that identical (monozygotic) twins have the same sets of genes as each other, then one can estimate a statistic known as 'heritability' for a certain trait by gauging whether identical twins are more similar to each other on a particular trait than fraternal twins. Reasonably high levels of heritability have been found for extraversion and neuroticism (emotional stability), where on the whole, the evidence indicates that over half of the variance in the human population on each of these traits can be attributed to genetic factors (Henderson, 1982). Of course, some caution remains as to the extent to which we can accept that twins represent the population as a whole or whether fraternal and identical twins have similar shared environmental experiences. Moreover, recent epigenetic research indicates there are subtle biological differences even between two identical twins, implying that personality differences between identical twins may not be completely explained by differences in their environments (Fraga et al., 2005).

Even with these caveats, research conducted on identical twins who have been adopted at birth has been impressive. There is evidence that for traits like extraversion and emotional stability, identical twins separated at birth due to adoption are more alike on these traits than fraternal twins who are brought up together (Pedersen et al., 1988). Findings such as these indicate that for certain traits biological maturation plays a big role in determining their expression, perhaps an even a bigger role than the environment in which a person is brought up. Research on babies also supports the view that there are temperamental differences between individuals even from birth and that these show relatively good stability during the early years. It has been shown that active and sociable babies are predisposed to developing extraversion traits, whereas irritable babies have an increased chance of becoming children and adults with lower emotional stability when compared with more placid babies (Rothbart, Ahadi and Evans, 2000).

Nevertheless, findings such as these should never lead us down the path of determinism. Acknowledging that we each start out with temperamental blueprints at birth does not mean that our destiny is fixed. In fact, far from this, evidence shows that people's environments really do matter over the course of their lives in shaping how personality becomes stable as well as how it can change over different life phases. Even if we adopt the view that there has to be a certain degree of important intra-individual stability in traits, it would be naive to ignore that personality development involves changes as well as continuities in personality over the lifespan. Although the Big Five traits in adults are at least moderately consistent over two periods of testing separated by a few years, it is clear that some traits (neuroticism, extraversion and openness) have better consistency than others (agreeableness and conscientiousness), and none of the correlations are perfect. Moreover the longer the gap between time intervals the lower the consistency of trait scores over the time period, indicating that people do have personality patterns but these can be amenable to a considerable degree of change and development. Modern longitudinal behavioural genetic research confirms that there are both genetic and environmental factors influencing stable and less stable phases in personality across the lifespan, with both biology and environment playing an important role in patterns of instability until middle age and with environmental factors having cumulative effects (Kandler, 2012).

One way of appreciating the relationship between traits and experience is to consider social maturation as well as biological development. We know that overall mean levels of neuroticism generally decrease with age: perhaps this has to do with people's growing resilience in facing adversities as they get older; conscientiousness shows an increase from young to older adulthood. Perhaps this reflects the fact that learning how to behave in ways that lead to more successful goal attainment and social successes takes time and wisdom. A very disorganised youngster for example may need the experience of failure and setbacks to be able to appreciate the importance of acquiring self-regulation skills in order to experience success. When we look at traits outside the realm of the Big Five we see many examples of age influencing the degree to which a trait gets manifested. For example sensation-seeking reduces from adolescence to middle adulthood, whereas characteristics such as autonomy, independence and competence tend to increase as people get older, especially for women. Biological maturation may go part way towards accounting for these age trends, but there is evidence that social and cultural experiences play important roles too, and for some traits social experiences probably play the biggest role. For example historical records inform us that for American women, their level of assertiveness increased as a function of greater participation in the workforce during the Second World War and fell again during those periods when they were expected to adopt more domestic roles during the 1950s and 1960s (Twenge, 2001).

Recent research has shown that contrary to the view that people's personalities stabilise during middle age, there is evidence of personality change even in old age. There is evidence that such changes are triggered by life challenges that typically occur in mature adulthood, such as retirement, loss of loved ones and adapting to physical limitations associated with getting old (Jackson et al., 2012). Whatever perspective a personality researcher wishes to adopt, a complete picture of a person's personality needs to accommodate the fact that, for each individual, development occurs from conception through to old age and that bidirectional influences between experience and inborn predispositions will shape the way personality unfolds across the lifespan.

The question remains as to how much people can change. Can an introvert ever really turn into a genuine extravert or does the introvert just learn to behave in ways that simulate extraverted behaviour without ever really altering his or her natural propensity towards introversion? This is one of the big questions that still cannot be answered. Some research suggests that simply acting more extraverted, conscientious, agreeable and open leads to feelings of authenticity, implying that such changes can lead to fundamental changes rather than just superficial ones (Fleeson and Wilt, 2010). A more ethical question might be whether one should even consider trying to change one's most natural traits to characteristics that are regarded to be desirable within a particular society. In fact, some evidence points to the benefits of certain traits that are not usually embraced. For example extraverts are often considered to be good communicators as they are assertive and sociable. Yet, people who are 'ambiverted' (neither extremely extraverted nor introverted) have been shown to make the better salespeople (Grant, 2013). Perhaps being ambiverted makes someone less verbally overbearing than a strong extravert. In fact, empathic listening is important for successful communication in many contexts, and in one study, when all Big Five traits were measured, extraversion was unrelated to empathic listening, whereas traits of agreeableness and openness were found to be important (Sims, 2016).

A different approach to embracing personality variability is to encourage people to make the most of what they already do best. The next section discusses one major outlook that is already addressing these issues about individual differences – namely the positive psychology approach.

How can we develop a flourishing personality?

It has probably not gone without notice that traditional personality theories (the psycho-dynamic tradition in particular) have a tendency to lean towards the dark side of people. In fact, a clinical focus is still a strong bias in the field of personality research. Just do a 'Google Scholar' search on personality in the last five years: psychopathology, crime, narcissism, borderline personality, depression, addiction and suicide appear quite frequently. Clearly, there is still a fascination with the dark and the dangerous.

The benefits of acquiring knowledge about how personality can be flawed should not be underestimated. Continuing to find ways of recognising people whose personalities are taking them down risky life paths is invaluable, and the development of efficacious interventions for personality disorders is an important focus of inquiry and investigation. Nevertheless, the time is finally here to redress the balance. Positive psychology does just this by concentrating on people's personal strengths and the way that healthy personalities promote happy and flourishing lives.

Although positive psychology is considered a fairly modern approach, it strongly echoes the key message of a more established school of thought – namely the humanistic school. The basic premise of the humanistic perspective is that all people are motivated to reach their full potential. From the late 1950s, Abraham Maslow and Carl Rogers drove a positive psychology agenda that had at its core the goal of moving people towards growth through a process they named self-actualisation. Humanistic psychology emphasises the goals for which people strive, their awareness of this striving and the importance of rational choice in this process. Self-actualised people encounter peak experiences, or moments of intense joy, awe and ecstasy.

In spite of starting off with some initial conflict, it soon became apparent to many that both humanistic and modern-day positive psychologists share very similar ambitions – namely that of explaining what makes people lead fully functioning, purposeful and successful lives. The main differences usually lie in choice of methodology. Positive psychologists generally emphasise scientific approaches to investigation, such as assessments, objective measurement and quantitative research methodology, whereas the humanistic psychologists originate from the idiographic camp and prefer qualitative methodology and phenomenological inquiry over experimental approaches and quantitative methods. For a humanistic theorist, what each individual experiences makes up a person's unique individuality and two people with similar backgrounds can have very different experiences of the same event. Carl Rogers argued that the meanings people bring to their life experiences are personal and subjective (Rogers, 1980). Therefore those who have criticised the humanistic school have mostly been psychologists who want to see a more evidence-based approach in order to acknowledge objective truths and make predictions yielding practical significance.

Perhaps the best solution for reconciling these conceptual differences is a mixed-methods approach. A combination of objective measurement and in-depth investigation can help to promote the identification of universal personality dimensions, while at the same time appreciating and encouraging the use of individualised developmental pathways. Indeed, in a coaching context, strengths and traits are considered from the personalised life history and autobiographical perspective of the coachee. This approach is likely to yield a much richer and more useful way of applying positive psychology to personality growth within the context of working towards individually valued personal and professional goals.

Positive psychology can tell us something about the traits that improve our well-being. This is where our old faithful, the extravert, gets the thumbs up yet again. It seems he or she is happier (Costa and McCrae, 1980; Tellegen, 1985; Pavot, Diener and Fujita, 1990; Headey and Wearing, 1992). However, research has revealed that traits such as 'optimism' and 'hope' are particularly beneficial in not only increasing one's happiness but also producing more successful relationships (Brissette, Scheier and Carver, 2002; Srivastava et al., 2006; Parker et al., 2014), improving work performance and/or engagement (Riolli and Savicki, 2003; Ouweneel et al., 2012) and even enhancing health and wellness (Scheier and Carver, 1987, 1992; Scioli et al., 1997; Lobel et al., 2000).

People who score higher on measures of 'flow' (the experience of complete absorption in the present moment), a term that was first coined and investigated by Mihaly Csikszentmihalyi (1990), are found to do better at school (Carli, Delle Fave and Massimini, 1988) and are more satisfied at work (Bryce and Haworth, 2002). In relation to flow, Nakamura and Csikszentmihalyi (2002) have also introduced the concept of an 'autotelic personality' (a person who tends to do things for their own sake rather than to achieve some later goal).

Identifying positive personality traits that produce optimal outcomes is good news for everyone, because positive theories of motivation focus on basic human needs for growth. It means that we all have the potential to self-actualise if we can remove those obstacles to flourishing. Edward Deci and Richard Ryan (2011) have produced a plethora of research findings based on their self-determination model. Essentially, the theory argues that people grow when they are intrinsically motivated and 'autonomously' driven (rather than driven by social expectations), when they experience 'competence' (rather than feeling failure) and when they feel they can engage with and experience meaningful relationships with other people. Such a motivational model implies that personality has more to do with the strategies people choose in meeting these three basic needs. Personalities can be seen as habitual patterns of thinking, feeling and interacting with the world driven by motives. For example a student who is driven to please others, avoid failure and maintain ongoing contact with people through social media may choose procrastination over task engagement. Lacking an intrinsic interest in a task along with the pursuit of such extrinsic rewards will make it difficult for this student to pursue focused self-regulated academic task engagement (Sims, 2014). One personality trait has been shown to identify people who persevere for long periods of time by putting in the effort for achieving goals that they are passionate about is the personality trait of 'grit' (Duckworth, 2016). One of the promising aspects of discovering traits such as grit is that the evidence shows that there are many possibilities for intervention. People can get grittier given the right kind of support and opportunities to identify with goals that are important to them, to recognise that traits are not fixed and to appreciate the importance of persistence and effort for attaining successful outcomes in life.

One of the biggest contributions that positive psychology has made to individual differences is the research on people's strengths. Martin Seligman and Chris Peterson (Peterson and Seligman, 2004) created a classification of universal core virtues that humans morally value regardless of their culture. From this they developed a set of 24 character traits that can be grouped under each of those core virtues. Park, Peterson and Seligman (2004) found that particular character strengths (hope, zest, gratitude and love) were positively associated with life satisfaction. Overall research in this area has highlighted the importance of identifying one's own strengths and using them in new ways and situations in one's daily life in order to achieve lasting happiness and success. For example a study of college students found that those who used their signature strengths made more progress in reaching their goals (Linley et al., 2010).

We are living through a period of political unrest, international crimes of extreme violence, economic uncertainties and cuts to our National Health Service. It would be perverse to strive for happiness without recognising the need to end suffering. Evidence is emerging to show that positive psychology interventions can be beneficial to clinical populations. In one study, depressed individuals who spent several weeks reading about strategies for increasing their satisfaction across various life domains no longer met the criteria for clinical depression at the end of the study (Grant et al., 1995). Another promising area has been research on post-traumatic growth (Tedeschi and Calhoun, 2004), the phenomenon that some people become stronger and create a more meaningful life in the wake of staggering adversity, such as war, illness or loss. This research extends the concept of resilience as bouncing back to resilience as bouncing forwards, where for example people who experience trauma become better individuals for overcoming it, handling it or accepting the consequences. Good examples of this are people who, as a result of their illness, become powerful advocates for others suffering the same fate. Positive change is commonly reported in around 30% to 70% of survivors of various traumatic events, including transportation or traffic accidents, natural disasters, combat, sexual abuse, medical problems, family breakdown, bereavement and immigration (Linley and Joseph, 2004). Therefore, while positive psychology set out to redress the balance by focusing on the 'bright' side, it is also contributing to the development of new insights into those areas that reflect individual differences in adverse conditions and circumstances.

What does psychology tell us about 'personality'?

This chapter has summarised major psychological approaches to understanding personality, each of which tells us something different about what personality is. Whether we see personality traits as measurable constructs or unique individual characteristics will ultimately depend on the research question we are asking. However, the goal for understanding personality should be to regard different approaches as complimentary. Focusing on conscious decision making and self-report may be useful in answering some questions, but the responsible researcher needs to remain open to the possibilities of influences on personality that are outside of awareness. Furthermore, while our biology may have provided us with the temperamental and neurological foundations for shaping our personality, an individual's personal set of experiences within a unique set of environmental contexts is likely to have a prevailing influence on those early dispositions. In fact, one's personality profile can change with age. Certainly, personality assessment at one point in time should never be exploited as a simple tool for labelling people, even if it can be informative about people's preferences, interests and communicative styles. Having a trait increases the likelihood of behaving in a consistent way. It does not mean that the person is compelled to behave in a particular way across all spheres and stages of his or her life.

Applied researchers will want to use the theories and techniques developed by psychologists to make decisions and predictions about people's preferences and behaviours within their particular fields of inquiry. This raises important questions. How do we develop resources and products that lead to the development of flourishing personalities? Do we fit people into jobs that are compatible with the attitudes, preferences and styles of people who have particular traits? Are productive leaders more inclined to relate to the strengths and goals of the employees and clients as well as the products of the organisation? Which people have communication styles suited to working with particular colleagues and customers? Are we producing resources that are capturing the attention of those people who could benefit from them the most? Does the personality of the designer influence the work he or she produces? Do certain traits influence how successful marketers become? Which customer traits do we need to be looking for when targeting our product?

Innovative research by applied investigators and practitioners from various fields must fully embrace the knowledge and research on personality that have been developed by psychologists over many years. In this regard, understanding individual differences in personality traits can be considered an extremely valuable means of progressing towards a healthier and more resourceful society that considers the nuanced needs, interests, beliefs, preferences, goals, strengths and values of the many individuals who live within it.

References

Adler, A. (1924). *The practice and theory of individual psychology*. Oxford: Harcourt, Brace.

Allport, G. W. and Odbert, H. S. (1936). Trait-names: A psycho-lexical study. *Psychological Monographs, 47*(1), pp. i–171.

Barlett, C. P. and Anderson, C. A. (2012). Direct and indirect relations between the big 5 personality traits and aggressive and violent behaviour. *Personality and Individual Differences, 52*, pp. 870–875.

Block, J. (1995). A contrarian view of the five-factor approach to personality description. *Psychological Bulletin, 117*(2), pp. 187–215.

Brissette, I., Scheier, M. F. and Carver, C. S. (2002). The role of optimism in social network development, coping, and psychological adjustment during a life transition. *Journal of Personality and Social Psychology, 82*(1), pp. 102–111.

Bryce, J. and Haworth, J. (2002). Wellbeing and flow in sample of male and female office workers. *Leisure Studies, 21*(3–4), pp. 249–263.

Buss, D. M. and Greiling, H. (1999). Adaptive individual differences. *Journal of Personality, 67*(2), pp. 209–243.

Carli, M., Fave, A. D. and Massimini, F. (1988). The quality of experience in the flow channels: Comparison of Italian and US students. In M. Csikszentmihalyi and I. S. Csikszentmihalyi (eds.), *Optimal experience: Psychological studies of flow in consciousness*. New York: Cambridge University Press, pp. 288–306.

Cattell, R. B. (1943). The description of personality: Basic traits resolved into clusters. *The Journal of Abnormal and Social Psychology, 38*(4), pp. 476–506.

Cattell, R. B., Eber, H. W. and Tatsuoka, M. M. (1970). *Handbook for the sixteen personality factor questionnaire (16 PF): In clinical, educational, industrial, and research psychology, for use with all forms of the test*. Champaign, IL: Institute for Personality and Ability Testing.

Chamorro-Premuzic, T. and Furnham, A. (2003). Personality predicts academic performance: Evidence from two longitudinal university samples. *Journal of Research in Personality, 37*(4), pp. 319–338.

Cheng, H. and Furnham, A. (2003). Personality, self-esteem, and demographic predictions of happiness and depression. *Personality and Individual Differences, 34*(6), pp. 921–942.

Cheung, F. M., van de Vijver, F. J. and Leong, F. T. (2011). Toward a new approach to the study of personality in culture. *American Psychologist, 66*(7), pp. 593–603.

Correa, T., Hinsley, A. W. and De Zuniga, H. G. (2010). Who interacts on the Web? The intersection of users' personality and social media use. *Computers in Human Behavior, 26*(2), pp. 247–253.

Costa Jr, P. T. and McCrae, R. R. (1980). Influence of extraversion and neuroticism on subjective well-being: Happy and unhappy people. *Journal of Personality and Social Psychology*, *38*(4), pp. 668–678.

Costa Jr, P. T. and McCrae, R. R. (1995). Domains and facets: Hierarchical personality assessment using the Revised NEO Personality Inventory. *Journal of Personality Assessment*, *64*(1), pp. 21–50.

Csikszentmihalyi, M. (1990). *Flow: The psychology of optimal performance*. New York: Cambridge University Press.

Deci, E. L. and Ryan, R. M. (2011). Self-determination theory. *Handbook of Theories of Social Psychology*, *1*, pp. 416–433.

Duckworth, A. (2016). *Grit: The power of passion and perseverance*. London: Vermilion.

Egan, S. and Stelmack, R. M. (2003). A personality profile of Mount Everest climbers. *Personality and Individual Differences*, *34*(8), pp. 1491–1494.

Ellis, A. (2004). *Rational emotive behavior therapy: It works for me – it can work for you*. Amherst, NY: Prometheus Books.

Erikson, E. H. and Erikson, J. M. (1998). *The life cycle completed (extended version)*. London: W.W. Norton.

Eysenck, H. J. (1967). *The biological basis of personality* (Vol. 689). London: Transaction.

Fleeson, W. (2001). Toward a structure- and process-integrated view of personality: Traits as density distributions of states. *Journal of Personality and Social Psychology*, *80*(6), pp. 1011–1027.

Fleeson, W. and Wilt, J. (2010). The relevance of big five trait content in behavior to subjective authenticity: Do high levels of within-person behavioral variability undermine or enable authenticity achievement? *Journal of Personality*, *78*(4), pp. 1353–1382.

Fraga, M. F., Ballestar, E., Paz, M. F., Ropero, S., Setien, F., Ballestar, M. L., Heine-Suñer, D., Cigudosa, J. C., Urioste, M., Benitez, J., Boix-Chornet, M., Sanchez-Aguilera, A., Ling, C., Carlsson, E., Poulsen, P., Vaag, A., Stephan, Z., Spector, T. D., Wu, Y, Z., Plass, C. and Esteller, M. (2005). Epigenetic differences arise during the lifetime of monozygotic twins. *Proceedings of the National Academy of Sciences of the United States of America*, *102*(30), pp. 10604–10609.

Freud, A. (1936). *The ego and the mechanisms of defence*. London: Hogarth.

Freud, S. (1960). *The ego and the id*, translated by Joan Riviere. New York: W.W. Norton.

Fromm, E. (1947). *Man for himself: An inquire into the psychology of ethics*. New York: Holt.

Funder, D. C. (2010). *The personality puzzle*. 5th ed., New York: Norton.

Goldberg, L. R. (1990). An alternative "description of personality": The big-five factor structure. *Journal of Personality and Social Psychology*, *59*(6), pp. 1216–1229.

Granö, N., Virtanen, M., Vahtera, J., Elovainio, M. and Kivimäki, M. (2004). Impulsivity as a predictor of smoking and alcohol consumption. *Personality and Individual Differences*, *37*(8), pp. 1693–1700.

Grant, A. M. (2013). Rethinking the extraverted sales ideal the ambivert advantage. *Psychological Science*, *24*(6), pp. 1024–1030.

Grant, G. M., Salcedo, V., Hynan, L. S., Frisch, M. B. and Puster, K. (1995). Effectiveness of quality of life therapy for depression. *Psychological Reports*, *76*(3c), pp. 1203–1208.

Grotstein, J. S. (1991). An American view of the British psychoanalytic experience: Psychoanalysis in counterpoint: The contributions of the British Object Relations School. *Melanie Klein and Object Relations*, *9*(2), pp. 34–62.

Hampson, S. E., Goldberg, L. R., Vogt, T. M. and Dubanoski, J. P. (2006). Forty years on: Teachers' assessments of children's personality traits predict self-reported health behaviors and outcomes at midlife. *Health Psychology*, *25*(1), pp. 57–64.

Headey, B. and Wearing, A. J. (1992). *Understanding happiness: A theory of subjective well-being*. Melbourne: Longman Cheshire.

Hellmuth, J. C. and McNulty, J. K. (2008). Neuroticism, marital violence, and the moderating role of stress and behavioral skills. *Journal of Personality and Social Psychology*, *95*(1), pp. 166–180.

Henderson, N. D. (1982). Human behavior genetics. *Annual Review of Psychology*, *33*(1), pp. 403–440.

Horney, K. (2000). *The unknown Karen Horney: Essays on gender, culture, and psychoanalysis*, edited by B. J. Paris. Newhaven, CT: Yale University Press.

Jackson, J. J., Hill, P. L., Payne, B. R., Roberts, B. W. and Stine-Morrow, E. A. (2012). Can an old dog learn (and want to experience) new tricks? Cognitive training increases openness to experience in older adults. *Psychology and Aging*, *27*(2), pp. 286–292.

Jung, C. G. (1923). *Psychological types: Or the psychology of individuation*. Oxford: Harcourt, Brace.

Jung, C. G. (1963). *Memories, dreams and reflections*, recorded and edited by A. Jaffé, translated by R. Winston and C. Winston, revised. New York: Vintage, Random House.

Kandler, C. (2012). Nature and nurture in personality development the case of neuroticism and extraversion. *Current Directions in Psychological Science*, *21*(5), pp. 290–296.

Kelly, G. A. (2003). A brief introduction to personal construct theory. In F. Fransella (ed.), *International handbook of personal construct psychology*. Chichester, UK: John Wiley, pp. 3–21.

Linley, P. A. and Joseph, S. (2004). Positive change following trauma and adversity: A review. *Journal of Traumatic Stress*, *17*(1), pp. 11–21.

Linley, P. A., Nielsen, K. M., Gillett, R. and Biswas-Diener, R. (2010). Using signature strengths in pursuit of goals: Effects on goal progress, need satisfaction, and well-being, and implications for coaching psychologists. *International Coaching Psychology Review*, *5*(1), pp. 6–15.

Lobel, M., DeVincent, C. J., Kaminer, A. and Meyer, B. A. (2000). The impact of prenatal maternal stress and optimistic disposition on birth outcomes in medically high-risk women. *Health Psychology*, *19*(6), pp. 544–553.

Malone, J. C., Cohen, S., Liu, S. R., Vaillant, G. E. and Waldinger, R. J. (2013). Adaptive midlife defense mechanisms and late-life health. *Personality and Individual Differences*, *55*(2), pp. 85–89.

McAdams, D. P. (1992). The five-factor model in personality: A critical appraisal. *Journal of Personality*, *60*(2), pp. 329–361.

McCrae, R. R. and Costa Jr, P. T. (2008). Empirical and theoretical status of the five-factor model of personality traits. In G. Boyle, G. Matthews and D. H. Saklofske, eds., *SAGE handbook of personality theory and assessment*, vol. 1. London: SAGE, pp. 273–294.

Miller, J. D., Lynam, D., Zimmerman, R. S., Logan, T. K., Leukefeld, C. and Clayton, R. (2004). The utility of the five factor model in understanding risky sexual behavior. *Personality and Individual Differences*, *36*(7), pp. 1611–1626.

Mischel, W. and Shoda, Y. (1995). A cognitive-affective system theory of personality: Reconceptualizing situations, dispositions, dynamics, and invariance in personality structure. *Psychological Review*, *102*(2), pp. 246–268.

Myers, I. B., McCaulley, M. H. and Most, R. (1985). *Manual: A guide to the development and use of the Myers-Briggs type indicator*. Palo Alto, CA: Consulting Psychologists Press.

Nakamura, J. and Csikszentmihalyi, M. (2002). The concept of flow. In C. R. Snyder and S. J. Lopez (eds.), *Handbook of positive psychology*. Oxford, UK: Oxford University Press, pp. 89–105.

Nettle, D. (2006). The evolution of personality variation in humans and other animals. *American Psychologist*, *61*(6), pp. 622–631.

Ouweneel, E., Le Blanc, P. M., Schaufeli, W. B. and van Wijhe, C. I. (2012). Good morning, good day: A diary study on positive emotions, hope, and work engagement. *Human Relations*, *65*(9), pp. 1129–1154.

Ozer, D. J. and Benet-Martinez, V. (2006). Personality and the prediction of consequential outcomes. *Annual Review of Psychology*, *57*, pp. 401–421.

Park, N., Peterson, C. and Seligman, M. E. (2004). Strengths of character and well-being. *Journal of Social and Clinical Psychology*, *23*(5), pp. 603–619.

Parker, P. D., Ciarrochi, J., Heaven, P., Marshall, S., Sahdra, B. and Kiuru, N. (2014). Hope, friends, and subjective well-being: A social network approach to peer group contextual effects. *Child Development*, *86*(2), pp. 642–650.

Pavot, W., Diener, E. and Fujita, F. (1990). Extraversion and happiness. *Personality and Individual Differences*, *11*(12), pp. 1299–1306.

Pedersen, N. L., Plomin, R., McClearn, G. E. and Friberg, L. (1988). Neuroticism, extraversion, and related traits in adult twins reared apart and reared together. *Journal of Personality and Social Psychology*, *55*(6), pp. 950–957.

Peterson, C. and Seligman, M. E. (2004). *Character strengths and virtues: A handbook and classification*. New York: Oxford University Press.

Reason, J. (2000). The Freudian slip revisited. *The Psychologist, British Psychological Society*, *13*(12), pp. 610–611.

Richardson, M., Abraham, C. and Bond, R. (2012). Psychological correlates of university students' academic performance: A systematic review and meta-analysis. *Psychological Bulletin*, *138*(2), pp. 353–387.

Riolli, L. and Savicki, V. (2003). Optimism and coping as moderators of the relation between work resources and burnout in information service workers. *International Journal of Stress Management*, *10*(3), pp. 235–252.

Rogers, C. (1980). *Way of being*. Boston: Houghton Mifflin.

Rothbart, M. K., Ahadi, S. A. and Evans, D. E. (2000). Temperament and personality: Origins and outcomes. *Journal of Personality and Social Psychology*, *78*(1), pp. 122–135.

Runyan, W. M. (1983). Idiographic goals and methods in the study of lives. *Journal of Personality*, *51*(3), pp. 413–437.

Sagiv, L. and Roccas, S. (2000). Traits and values: The five factor model and the Schwartz value theory. *International Journal of Psychology*, *35*(3–4).

Scheier, M. F. and Carver, C. S. (1987). Dispositional optimism and physical well-being: The influence of generalized outcome expectancies on health. *Journal of Personality*, *55*(2), pp. 169–210.

Scheier, M. F. and Carver, C. S. (1992). Effects of optimism on psychological and physical well-being: Theoretical overview and empirical update. *Cognitive Therapy and Research*, *16*(2), pp. 201–228.

Scioli, A., Chamberlin, C. M., Samor, C. M., Lapointe, A. B., Campbell, T. L., Macleod, A. R. and McLenon, J. (1997). A prospective study of hope, optimism, and health. *Psychological Reports*, *81*(3), pp. 723–733.

Silverthorne, C. (2001). Leadership effectiveness and personality: A cross cultural evaluation. *Personality and Individual Differences*, *30*(2), pp. 303–309.

Sims, C. (2014). Self-regulation coaching to alleviate student procrastination: Addressing the likeability of studying behaviours. *International Coaching Psychology Review*, *9*(2), pp. 147–164.

Sims, C. (2016). Do the big-five personality traits predict empathic listening and assertive communication? *International Journal of* Listening, *28*, pp. 1–26.

Srivastava, S., McGonigal, K. M., Richards, J. M., Butler, E. A. and Gross, J. J. (2006). Optimism in close relationships: How seeing things in a positive light makes them so. *Journal of Personality and Social Psychology*, *91*(1), pp. 143–153.

Tedeschi, R. G. and Calhoun, L. G. (2004). Posttraumatic growth: Conceptual foundations and empirical evidence. *Psychological Inquiry*, *15*(1), pp. 1–18.

Tellegen, A. (1985). Structures of mood and personality and their relevance to assessing anxiety, with an emphasis on self-report. In A. H. Tuma and J. D Maser (eds.), *Anxiety and the anxiety disorders*. Hillsdale, NJ: Erlbaum, pp. 681–706.

Twenge, J. M. (2001). Birth cohort changes in extraversion: A cross-temporal meta-analysis, 1966–1993. *Personality and Individual Differences*, *30*(5), pp. 735–748.

Watson, D. C. (2001). Procrastination and the five-factor model: A facet level analysis. *Personality and Individual Differences*, *30*(1), pp. 149–158.

Part I

Personality encoded in graphic expression

Chapter 2

Personality and graphic expression

Gloria Moss

The impact of personality on graphic expression

Without design and marketing it is difficult to see how many businesses would survive. Marketing is in many ways an umbrella term that embraces design, with design impacting on the four elements in the marketing mix of product, place, price and promotion and shaping a person's overall reactions to a product (Roy and Wield, 1989). The central questions of this book concerns the extent to which personality impacts on design and marketing *creations* and *reactions* to these creations, and this chapter focuses on *creations*, with *preferences* the focus of a later chapter.

Surprisingly given the importance of design and marketing, there has been relatively little research looking specifically at the links between these disciplines and personality and this is the prompt to this book. In this chapter, the spotlight is shone on the extent to which personality is expressed in people's visual *creations*, drawing on studies focused on graphic expression rather than design and marketing and conducted over a fairly long timescale. Even recently, prominent commentators were making fairly general comments on the links between personality and design creations, with Deyan Sudjic, for example, director of London's Design Museum, writing of design as a 'reflection of emotional and cultural values' (2009, p. 49).

So, this chapter reaches back into the past to reveal a rich vein of studies examining the links between personality and graphic expression, highlighting principles that can, given evidence for the consistency of all graphic expression, be applied across to design and marketing. The reader will notice that much of this research was conducted in the relatively distant past, when there appeared to be an appetite for exploring the links binding a piece of graphic expression to the personality of its creator, and this work has not, to the best of our knowledge, been brought together in one place before and has not been directed at those interested in the applications of this knowledge to design and marketing.

This is to be regretted since, as we shall see, there is a rich vein of research exploring the links between art, design and their creators. The findings of this work, as we shall see, is summarised nicely by Alfred Tunnelle's pithy view that the artist is someone who sees things not as they are but as he is (Hammer, 1980, p. 8). It should be noted that this remark appears in a book devoted to projective drawings, and we should not be surprised to find this view expressed there since there is a body of research that views the process of drawing or designing as one of projection in which the drawing or design serves as an X-ray image of its creator.

Of course, fundamental to the relevance of this work to design and marketing is the notion that different forms of graphic expression, be they paintings, drawings or designs, are allied forms of graphic expression, something that would allow findings in one discipline (say, painting or digital drawings) to be extrapolated to a discipline such as design. So the first issue considered in detail relates to the extent to which different visual forms are consistent with each other. This is the subject of the next section.

The consistency of different forms of graphic expression: theory

A key question in cross-disciplinary research in the visual sphere relates to the extent to which design and other forms of graphic expression, such as fine art, are connected. Historically, many of the divisions between visual disciplines that we are familiar with today were absent in the past. So for example design was referred to in decades past as 'commercial art' and the first professional organisation of designers in Britain in 1930 was called the Society of Industrial Artists. Relatedly, in 1934 George Nelson, one of America's most cerebral designers (Sudjic, 2009), claimed that 'the designer is in essence an artist, one whose tools differ somewhat from those of his predecessors, but an artist nonetheless' (Buchanan, 1995, p. 54). A few decades later, the question was explored by Herbert Read (1953) in his book *Art and Industry*, where he argued that any distinction between art and design was the creation of the machine age, with his arguments rooted in historical as well as aesthetic data. For example he draws attention to the fact that in classical Greece, a single word 'techne' was used to cover pure and applied art and, prior to the Renaissance, arts that we would currently define as 'fine arts' (architecture, sculpture, painting, music and poetry) were not recognised as separate disciplines. Moreover, he goes on to argue that 'applied arts' (i.e. objects designed primarily for use) appeal to aesthetic sensibilities in the same way that abstract art does and that in both cases, there is an intuitive as well as a rational element that allows them to satisfy the canons of beauty.

The question of the relationship between artistic disciplines has not gone away. So, recently it was taken up by Buchanan (1995), who referred to Read's work as a 'standard text' in the US and Britain and 'an exceptionally influential introductory work on design for general readers' (Buchanan, 1995, p. 51). Where the fine arts are concerned, Buchanan considers that one of the three elements that contribute to the development of design in the contemporary world is an awareness of the aesthetic appeal of forms, and he sees no contradiction in the notion of design as a cognitive and expressive skill. In fact, in his words, 'expression *is* design thinking' (ibid., p. 46) and he quotes approvingly George Nelson's vision of design as 'communication and of the designer as artist' (ibid., p. 54), making a persuasive case for design as an expressive skill. To quote from his work, 'Leonardo da Vinci's speculations on mechanical devices were simply another expression of his poetic and visual imagination' (ibid., p. 33). Walter Gropius's goal, likewise, was to 'provide a concrete connection between artistic exploration and practical action' (ibid., p. 37). In fact, most designers recognise that the appearance and expressive quality of products are critically important not only in marketing but also in the substantive contribution of design to daily living (ibid., p. 45). 'Expression does not clothe design thinking; it is design thinking in its most immediate manifestation, providing the integrative aesthetic experience which incorporates the array of technical decisions contained in any product' (ibid., p. 46). Read's and Buchanan's sentiments show that there is nothing in the finished work of design that sets it apart *per se* from the work of 'fine art', and the discipline of 'visual culture' is predicated on similar assumptions insofar as it blurs the boundaries between different visual disciplines. Here is Rogoff (1998) for example offering an explanation for the emergence of this unified approach to the visual arts: 'Images do not stay within discrete disciplinary fields such as "documentary film" or "Renaissance painting" since neither the eye nor the psyche operates along or recognises such divisions' (Rogoff, 1998, p. 26). Some might still claim that the functional nature of design sets it apart from the disciplines of painting and drawing, and while it may be true that most designers are more constrained than most fine artists, this is a difference of degree alone and a design brief will still afford the designer the scope for producing an individual response. As Buchanan (1995) points out,

> The subject of design is not given . . . the subject matter of design is radically indeterminate, open to alternative resolutions even within the same methodology . . . There are many constraints on the work of a designer but the consideration of constraints is only a background for the invention or conception of a new product.
> (Buchanan, 1995, pp. 24–25)

The same might also be said of handwriting, where, although literate individuals are taught a copybook, each person's handwriting is distinct from that of another. In fact, these departures from the copybook are what define the individual nature of a handwriting and so you can think of the copybook as analogous to the design brief insofar as it sets the parameters but still leaves room for movement. One has only to consider signatures and the way that these are admitted as evidence of a person's identity to realise how defining a mark of individuality these are. In this way, we can see that the copybook or design brief may place limits on the writer or designer but will always leave room for self-expression.

Some might also suggest that design is a discipline apart from drawing and painting and drawing on the basis of often being produced by a team rather than an individual, leaving little room for self-expression. However, just as there are exceptions to this rule, with some design work produced by individuals, so also are there cases where fine art has been produced by a team. This shows that the issue of whether the work is produced individually or in teams is a contextual rather than fundamental differentiator of design and fine art.

The consistency of different forms of graphic expression: evidence

In fact, a comparison of drawing, painting, handwriting and design shows that these are all forms of graphic expression and one might ask how great the consistency is across two or more of these disciplines. Fortunately, two attempts have been made to answer this question, the first in a 1933 study by Allport and Vernon (reprinted in 1967) and the second in a 1948 study by a psychology professor, Wolff. We will take a brief look at these two publications.

Allport is well-known for his 'influential personality' theory (Fancher, 1979) and his 'great' (Koch and Leary, 1992) book *Personality: A Psychological Interpretation* (1937). Just a few years before the publication of this book he had researched with Vernon the extent to which features of different motor acts inter-correlated (Allport and Vernon, 1933), with their findings based on experiments conducted with 25 male subjects. The study was conducted in four phases. In the first, subjects were given a pencil or crayon and an A4 writing surface and asked to draw the following figures:

Circles drawn on paper, with the right hand
Circles drawn on paper, with the left hand

Circles drawn with crayon, right and left hands
Squares drawn on blackboard, right hand
Squares drawn in sandbox, right and left feet
Parallel lines drawn on paper, right and left hands.

Inter-correlations between these six items were examined with respect to three elements (the average area of figures; the total areas occupied by the figures; the proportion of unoccupied space) and results are shown in Table 2.1.

That table shows the inter-correlations between the aforementioned factors, and you can see that levels of inter-correlations recorded are higher than 0.5, the minimum level for this number of subjects at which the results are statistically significant at the 0.01 level. If you consider that the different shapes depicted are examples of 'graphic expression' then these results evidence the presence of high levels of consistency between different forms of graphic expression produced by a single person.

Further research to establish whether different forms of graphic expression have unifying features in the work of a single person was conducted by Wolff, a psychology professor, 15 years later (1948). The focus this time was on handwriting and doodles with Wolff asking 20 female subjects to produce handwriting and shapes in four different conditions: using right and left hands and then with eyes open and then closed. Subjects were asked to produce a number of shapes: a horizontal line, a vertical line, a circle, a triangle, a square, a normal signature, signatures that were smaller and larger than usual and a disguised signature.

As noted, each form was produced in four settings and, according to Wolff, the chance probability of the four variations appearing in identical form in these varied settings was no more than 10%. Despite this, Wolff detected identical forms across the four settings in a massive 54% of cases, in other words in five times more cases than chance would have led one to expect. Wolff received similar results with male students and he went on to repeat the experiment a week later, with the consistencies this time appearing in 46% of the four settings. This led Wolff to conclude that there was 'a constancy of graphic expression under various unfamiliar conditions' (Wolff, 1948, p. 22) and an 'intricate relationship of consistencies' (Wolff, 1948, pp. 23–24).

Wolff's results appear to offer convincing evidence to support this final claim and they appear to corroborate Allport and Vernon's findings of a correspondence between different forms of graphic expression. A word of caution, however. Wolff refers to 'consistencies' between shapes and forms but does not define this term, thereby creating uncertainties as to precisely how similar shapes and forms must be before they are deemed to be 'consistent'. For this reason, the results of his experiment cannot be accepted uncritically.

It is fortunate for us that this was not Wolff's only experiment. He went on to question whether the consistency of graphic expression could be the result of imitation, learning and training rather than individual expression, testing the extent to which writers can disguise their handwriting. In order to put this question to the test, three subjects were

Table 2.1 Inter-correlations between the features contained in different forms, excluding the drawings done just with the left hand (Allport and Vernon, 1933).

Average area of figures	Total area occupied by the figure	Proportion of unoccupied space
0.87	0.74	0.71

asked to write a phrase in 'the usual' and in a 'disguised' way, as well as in capitals. A further group of three subjects was given the handwriting samples and asked to try to match the phrases to a single person. The results showed that subjects were able to distinguish the original from the disguised writing in 70% of cases, demonstrating that the personal impulses behind graphic expression cannot be easily disguised. The findings also show that even where people begin by being taught a copybook method of writing, they normally depart from it and create their own handwriting. These findings led Wolff to conclude that graphic expression is a personal expression of cognition.

A further experiment by Wolff illustrates this vividly. Wolff asked three subjects to produce handwriting ('Specimen A') as well as doodles ('Specimen B'). He then gave Specimens A and B to two separate groups of ten people, asking them to produce descriptions (Sets A and B) of the expressive qualities contained there. A further group of people was given Sets A and B and asked to match them so that a description related to Set A could be paired with a description from Set B. The results? While chance would produce matchings in just 15% (0.15) of cases the percentage of correct pairings of Sets A and B was 70% (0.7). This second experiment of Wolff's demonstrates, as does that of Allport and Vernon, that different forms of graphic expression are consistent with each other.

So we can see that the studies conducted by Allport and Vernon as well as by Wolff invite two conclusions. The first is that graphic expression bears the mark of its maker and the second is that different forms of graphic expression are consistent with each other. This second point implies that the features contained in someone's graphic expression – whether it be handwriting, doodles, drawings, paintings or designs – will always be internally consistent. This second point shows that personality inferences made in one field (e.g. drawings) can be used to predict findings in another field (e.g. designs). This opens up the field, in which the impact of personality on graphic expression can be studied.

The manifestation of personality in graphic expression

According to the psychologists Allport and Vernon, the motor acts which produce drawings and paintings 'must reflect to a large degree the organization of the total brain field' (1933, p. 181). They argued that the brain directs the hands of the writer and the artist so that the handwriting or paintings that they produce reflect aspects of their personality.

They were not alone in this view, with several other studies producing similar conclusions. One group of studies is focused around the 'draw-a-person' test, the topic of the next section. As we can see, this test produces results that suggest that people project themselves and their personalities into their drawings.

Draw-a-person test

The 1950s was a period in which several studies using the 'draw-a-person' test – one in which participants are invited to draw a person – were conducted. The first of these, by Weider and Noller (1953), found that 70%–74% of primary school boys and 94%–97% of girls drew their own sex first. This tendency was unrelated to socio-economic status. A further study at this time by Jolles (1952) found that around 80% of children aged 5–8 drew people of their own sex. In the same year, two studies by Knopf and Richards found a tendency for 80% of boys to draw someone of their own gender. In 1953 Mainord found that this tendency to draw someone of the same gender continued into adulthood, with a smaller proportion of women than men drawing a figure of their own sex first. In 1955, Tolor and Tolor found 82% of boys and 91% of girls drawing a person of their own sex. In 1958, out of a massive sample of 5,500 adults consisting of college students, high school students and psychiatric patients, 89% drew their own sex first. Excluding those who were patients in hospitals, 72% drew their own sex first (Hammer, 1980).

The finding that people tend to draw someone of their own gender emerged from four further studies. In 1960, Bieliauskas collected 1,000 drawings from people aged 4 to 14 and found that both sexes favoured their own sex when drawing a person. The tendency to do this increased with age, particularly after the age of nine, although the developmental pattern was more stable for boys than for girls (Cox, 1993). A second study by Tolor and Tolor (1974) showed more than 90% of girls and boys producing drawings of people of their own gender and two more recent studies produced similar conclusions. The first of these, by Papadakis-Michaelides (1989), found over 73% of boys and 78% of girls drawing their own sex, while a study in 1990 by Aronoff and McCormick of the drawing of 109 undergraduates found that males and masculine persons drew males first while female and feminine persons tended to draw females first; those with more androgynous characteristics were found to be equally likely to draw a male or a female first. A list of these studies is provided in Table 2.2, showing the number of respondents in each study, their age range and the percentage of boys and girls drawing their own gender first.

From this, it can be seen that several researchers or groups of researchers have found a significant tendency in the 'Draw a Person' test for own sex depictions. One might ask why this is. One theory is that the sex of the figure drawn reflects the sex role identity or sexual orientation of the artist (Aronoff and McCormick, 1990). Against that, there have been studies which call this interpretation into question. Brown and Tolor (1957) for example in an extensive review of the literature, doubt that choice of sex in figure drawing reflected the drawer's psychosexual identification or adjustment. An alternative theory advanced by a number of scholars is that the image drawn of the body is a configuration or gestalt of one's own body and that when individuals draw a person they may reflect the impression they have of their own body – or, if not of the body, then of a projection of aspects of oneself. As we saw at the beginning of the chapter, Alfred Tunnelle declared, 'The artist does not see things as they are but as he is' (Hammer, 1980, p. 8), and this explanation could underpin much

Table 2.2 Percentage of boys and girls drawing their own sex first.

Study	n	Age range	% boys	% girls
Weider and Noller, 1953	153	8–10	74	97
Weider and Noller, 1953	438	7–12	70	94
Knopf and Richards, 1952	20	6	80	50
Knopf and Richards, 1952	20	8	80	70
Jolles, 1952	2,560	5–12	85	80
Tolor and Tolor, 1955	136	9–12	82	91
Bieliaskas, 1960	1,000 drawings	4–14	71	73
Tolor and Tolor, 1974	232	10–12	91	94
Papadakis-Michaelidas, 1989	507	2; 6–11; 5	73.4	78.6
Aronoff and McCormick, 1990	109	Undergraduates	High proportion	High proportion

of what has been discussed thus far. For, if graphic expression communicates much about the person who has created it, this could be precisely because a person projects aspects of him- or herself into the graphic work he or she creates.

Graphic expression more generally

Where graphic expression more generally is concerned, five notable studies were conducted within 30 years of Allport and Vernon's study, producing similar conclusions. This was a period when there was a great interest in the links between graphic expression and personality, and two of the studies adopted a quantitative approach (Waehner, 1946; Aronson, 1958) and the others one that was more qualitative.

Waehner's study (1946) focused on the formal aspects of the drawings of nursery school pupils and college students (aged 17 and 19 years of age), producing personality descriptions of the 'artists' from an analysis of the features contained in the drawings and paintings analysed. Waehner then invited teachers (who knew the students) and psychologists (who carried out personality tests) to identify the subjects from these descriptions, and the results of the nursery school matchings showed a high degree of accuracy. In the case of the college students, the matches were correct in 68% of cases, as Table 2.3 shows.

These are impressive results. Waehner's descriptions of the personalities of the students and nursery school children were based exclusively on an application of a system of decoding personality from graphic expression. Table 2.4 shows some examples taken from Waehner's study.

Table 2.3 Percentage of correct identifications by teachers and psychologists of persons described anonymously (Waehner, 1946).

Subjects	% of judges with 100% correct matching	% of judges with only 80%	% of Waehner's descriptions correctly matched by judges
Nursery school children	80	20	85
College students	–	–	Average of 68

Table 2.4 Interpretation of generic features in drawings and paintings (Waehner, 1946).

Generic feature	Example	Interpretation
Size	Small size	Anxiety, depression, reduced energy, tendency to control
Distribution	Central distribution	Immature, depressive
	Symmetrical distribution	Conventional/depressive, controlled/constricted
	Wide distribution (over 50% of area)	Free imagination, relaxed mood, creative
Curved/sharp edges	< 50% curves and many sharp edges	Aggressive/offensive
	>70% curves and few sharp edges	Introverted, creative, restrained, preoccupied with self
Colour	Greater colour than form variety	Energy, impetus, initiative
	Greater form than colour variety	Intellectually better developed than emotionally controlled

A second study with quantifiable results was that of Aronson (1958) in which he investigated the graphic features corresponding with Murray's high achiever personality type known as nAch ('Need for achievement'). This personality type was defined by Murray in 1939 as pursuing long-term goals, being energetic and non-conforming and enjoying the pursuit of risks. Building on this concept, Aronson devised a projective test to allow a person's nAch to be measured from the shapes he or she depicted.

The subjects in Aronson's study were 196 male college students who had completed the Thematic Aperception Test (TAT), a personality instrument for testing nAch. After being shown a number of abstract shapes, the subjects were then divided into five groups and asked to reproduce from memory the shapes that they had viewed. Aronson then examined the association between the shapes and nAch TAT results from Group 1 and, on the basis of this, devised a scoring system which awarded high scores ('high') for high nAch and low scores ('low') for low nAch as follows:

1   Preponderance of single, unattached, discrete lines (high). The lines of the person with a low need for achievement are overlaid and fuzzy (low).
2   Diagonal forming an angle with a horizontal (high).
3   Two directional, non-repetitive lines (high).
4   Undulating lines consisting of two or more crests (high).

Aronson then scored the work of the students using this system, producing a total score, the so-called quartile score ('TQS'), with correlations as shown in Table 2.5.

It is interesting therefore to observe that three out of five of the correlations with the TAT (Groups III, IV and V) reached a high level of significance (p – < 0.01 level) and Group II reached a significance level of p = < 0.05. These results are statistically significant and suggest that a person's graphic expression can indeed afford insights into personality.

How valid are Aronson's results? In terms of test-retest reliability, the score-rescore correlation for Group V with the TQS was a high 0.93. In terms of inter-rater reliability, a high score of 0.89 was obtained regardless of which group's scores were retested, with the second assessor producing assessments independently of the first. In terms of validity, correlations between Aronson's test and the TAT were high, and this is significant given the respectable validity figures obtained independently for the TAT. In terms of detailed results, the mean validity coefficient between the judgement of 29 clinicians and 17 psychologists working with the TAT was 0.60, a highly significant result (Little and Schneidman, 1955).

Table 2.5 Correlation between criteria of graphic expression and TAT nAch score.

Group	N	Correlation between TQS and TAT results
I	26	0.41*
II	18	0.38*
III	26	0.62**
IV	51	0.37**
V	75	0.36**

Note: *p – 0<0.05 **p = <0.01 (Aronson, 1958).

So, Waehner's and Aronson's studies strongly suggest that personality can be inferred from graphic expression and, not surprisingly perhaps, a number of qualitative studies have reached the same conclusion. One by Alschuler and Hattwick (1947) presents an extended analysis of the paintings of 150 children aged two to four years in relation to what is known of their behaviours from history and progress records, teachers' daily logs and full-day diary records. This is an interesting study so it will be explored in some detail here.

In the course of their work, Alschuler and Hattwick discuss the significance of the use of colour, line and form, arguing for a link between colour and strong emotional drives and between line and form and self-control, concern with external stimuli and higher frequency of reasoned (in contrast to impulsive) behaviour. Where individual colours are concerned they argue that a concentration of red may signal the opposite of affection; blue sublimation or control; yellow dependency and emotional behaviour; green a lack of strong, overtly expressed emotions and black a dearth of emotional behaviour and repressed emotions.

Where shape is concerned, they note that children whose drawings emphasise straight lines tend to stand out for their relatively assertive, outgoing behaviour, with length of line corresponding with control and less impulsive behaviour. Those with curved, continuous strokes on the other hand are said to be more dependent, withdrawn, submissive and subjectively orientated than those forming vertical, square or rectangular forms.

Applying this understanding of colour and shape, Alschuler and Hattwick conclude that children tend to express through creative media the same feelings expressed in overt behaviour: 'almost every drawing and painting made by a young child is meaningful and in some measure expresses the child who did it' (1947, p. 5); 'children tend to draw and paint what they are feeling and experiencing rather than what they see' (ibid., p. 8). Alschuler and Hattwick's conclusions are interesting, but since they provide relatively few details of their methodology and offer no independent measure of the children's personality it is difficult to offer unreserved support for their conclusions. If, however, their results are compared with those of Waehner, there does appear to be consistency (see Table 2.6).

The fourth study was carried out by Herbert Read (1958), whose book *Art and Industry* (1953) we referred to earlier. In this book, he reports on his analysis of several thousand drawings from a variety of schools, identifying features there corresponding to the eight personality types defined by Jung. Unfortunately, as in Alschuler and Hattwick's study, there is

Table 2.6 Interpretation of graphic features by Waehner (1946) and Alschuler and Hattwick (1947).

Feature	Author	Interpretation of this feature by the author
Colour dominance	Waehner	Energy, impetus, initiative
	Alschuler	Strong emotional drives
Form dominance	Waehner	Better intellectual than emotional development; over-control
	Alschuler	Self-control, concern with external stimuli; high concentration of reasoned behaviour
Straight lines	Waehner	Aggression
	Alschuler	Assertive, outgoing behaviour
Curved lines	Waehner	Introverted, creative, self-centred
	Alschuler	Dependent, compliant, affectionate, fanciful imagination

Table 2.7 The personality types that produce different painterly characteristics (Read, 1958, pp. 92–3).

Personality types: extraverted	Personality types: introverted
Extravert Scene is objectively portrayed; realistic.	**Introvert** Maker conveys the impression that the object/scene made on him/her; subjective.
Thinking extravert The eye registers detail like a camera. The scene is fixed.	**Thinking introvert** The maker projects himself into the object. Expressionistic, vital and organic.
Sensing extravert Simplified but objective and realistic; representational.	**Sensing introvert** Subjective experience of reality but based on real rather than imaginary objects.
Feeling extravert Natural forms are embellished; decorative.	**Feeling introvert** Latent images of the unconscious; imaginative.
Intuitive extravert Apprehension of abstract proportion of relationships. Real scene but objects arranged in a rhythmical structure; geometric.	**Intuitive introvert** Pure, abstract and non-formal, spatial structure.

no external measure of the children's personality and no independent validation, therefore, of his findings. Notwithstanding these limitations, we report here the graphic features that, according to Read, characterise the different personality types (Table 2.7).

Read's results were published in 1958 and in the same year, Hammer published a related piece of work examining the connections between drawings and personality. Entitled *The Clinical Application of Projective Drawings* and reprinted in 1980, the book relates the pictures that people draw to aspects of their personality. In one chapter for example, 'Expressive Aspects of Projective Drawings', he summarises earlier attempts to interpret different drawing characteristics. Unfortunately, as with Read's and Alschuler and Hattwick's findings, there is no attempt to critically evaluate the results but a partial evaluation can be made through a comparison of the interpretations offered by different researchers, with a percentage estimation of researchers agreeing on a particular interpretation (see Table 2.8).

Although Hammer's summary does not present quantified results, the studies he quotes do appear to coalesce to a high extent in their conclusions.

Since Read's and Hammer's work lacks experimental rigour, an attempt was later made to test some of their conclusions and in an unpublished doctoral dissertation, Burt (1968) acknowledged that much of the previous work had been based on 'unreliable, subjective interpretations', something he attempted to rectify in his own study. In this, he obtained the Myers-Briggs Type Indicator (MBTI) set of personality types for 72 subjects (60 female and 12 male), with the majority showing as 'Intuitive' types. Each subject produced five oil paintings, which were classified by independent raters using six categories:

1   Colour (bright/dull; dark/light).
2   Line – clarity; whether defined or blurred.
3   Form; the degree of distortion.
4   Realism.
5   Detail.
6   Vitality.

Table 2.8 Summary of different research findings (adapted from Hammer, 1980).

Generic feature	Example	Researcher and interpretation offered	% agreement for a particular interpretation
Size	**Small**	Hammer (1980) – low self-esteem Traub – inferiority feelings (quoted in Hammer, p. 65) Lembke – inferiority feelings (quoted in Hammer, p. 65) Waehner (1946) – anxiety, shyness Alschuler and Hattwick (1947) – emotionally dependent behaviour Elkisch (1945) – feeling shut in	83% of researchers consider that small size is related to behaviour that is indicative of lack of confidence.
	Large	Hammer (1980) – high self-esteem, frustration and aggression Precker (1950) – aggression Zimmerman and Garfinkle (1942) – aggression	100% of researchers consider that large size points to confidence and aggression.
Pressure	**Light**	Hammer (1980) – low energy Alschuler and Hattwick (1947) – low energy or restraint Buck (1950) – depression	100% of researchers consider that weak pressure indicates low energy.
Quality of line	**Straight**	Alschuler and Hattwick (1947) – assertive Krout (1950) – aggressive moods	100% of researchers consider that straight lines point to assertiveness.
	Circular	Krout (1950) – femininity	Only one researcher
Detailing	**Great**	Brick (1944) – compulsive behaviour Alschuler and Hattwick (1947) – pedantic behaviour Hammer (1980) – pedantic behaviour	66% agreement.
Placing	**To the right**	Buck (1950) – controlled behaviour Koch and Leary (1992) – inhibition Wolff (1948) – introversion	100% agreement.

Note: Reference to the studies quoted here can be found in *The Clinical Application of Projective Drawings*, by E. F. Hammer, 1980, Springfield: Charles C. Thomas.

Burt found a significant correlation between painterly characteristics and personality type, in particular finding the following:

A. The paintings of superior function intuitives differed from those of other types in the following respects:
    a. Realism. Their paintings were less realistic (p = <0.07).
    b. Distortion of form. Their paintings showed more distortion of form (p= <0.02).
    c. Clarity of line. Their paintings had more clarity of line (p = <0.02).
    d. Colour. Their paintings were rated higher on surface colour than the other functions combined (p = <0.01).

Table 2.9 The association between MBTI type and design characteristics (Matthews et al., 2010).

Personality type	Design characteristics
Extravert	More direct-entry sequences, more open interior spaces and less separation between private and public space than introverts
Introverts	More likely to create indirect entry sequences, less open interior space and more separation between private and public space than extraverts
Sensing	Interiors categorised by order, symmetry and grid; were also more likely to create direct-entry sequences and shun texture richness
Intuitive	Favoured indirect entrances and texture richness
Thinking	Progression and grid were perceived to be organising principles and avoidance of colour warmth
Feeling	Avoided entrance transition rooms and tended to use warm colours
Judgement	Separated the public from the private and designed with a grid as an organising element
Perception	Likely to keep decisions open with public and private spaces directly accessible to one another

B. There were no significant differences between the paintings of introverts and extraverts.
C. 'Judging' types used rich colour and relatively undistorted forms while 'Perception' types used less rich colour and relatively distorted forms (p = <0.01); 'Judging' types were also more likely than 'Perception' types to use greater detail (p = <0.06).

Burt's findings are more precise than those of Read insofar as he not only used a well-validated personality instrument to test Jung's types (the MBTI) but also used independent raters to assess subjects' paintings. The fact that he chose the parameters against which the paintings would be assessed is also methodologically sound since the categories chosen are broad-based and followed an examination of the art creations. His findings, based as they are on a sound methodology, therefore give grounds for confidence, and it is noteworthy that four out of six of the results just quoted are statistically significant at the level of p = <0.05 or more. This shows that the chances of his results occurring by chance are no more than 7%.

Moving closer to the present day, a study by Matthews et al. (2010) examined the links between MBTI type and type of house design produced, with the results shown in Table 2.9. Interesting though this study is, a major limiting factor is the apparently arbitrary selection of the five rating categories used. There would have been a clearer rationale for the selection of rating characteristics has these not been created, as in Burt's study, following an examination of the completed designs.

Personality and graphic expression: conclusions

This overview of the literature suggests that there is strong evidence to support the notion that personality is manifested in graphic expression. Many of the studies evidencing this were conducted many decades ago when this subject attracted a great deal of research interest, and the age of the studies is relevant only insofar as the methodologies of some of the studies are lacking the rigour that might be expected in more modern studies. Mapping some of the less rigorous studies against those that are more rigorous does, however, reveal strong correlations, creating a body of work that collectively makes a strong case for the evidencing of personality in graphic expression.

Given the importance of design and marketing in today's world, an understanding of the critical role played by personality in shaping graphic expression highlights an individual factor of which organisations need to be aware. In the next section of the book, we will bring in the all-important perspective of the observer and the way that the observer's personality will influence preferences for graphic expression. A related and key question will concern the extent to which people of one personality type are drawn to graphic expression created by those of a similar personality disposition, a question with important implications for organisational recruitment and selection.

Meanwhile, in order to bring our understanding of the issues up to date, three chapters follow reporting on studies examining the link between graphic expression and personality conducted in more recent times. The first, by Bill Wylie (Chapter 3), looks at the way that drawings can convey information about their creators, in this case, in the context of therapeutic work in a prison. The second, by Professor Jim Blythe (Chapter 4), examines the extent to which an advertising creative's personality influences his or her professional output. Finally, Professor Judi Harris (Chapter 5) examines the all-important question of the extent to which digital graphics reveal the personalities of their creators.

References

Allport, G. W. (1937). *Personality: A Psychological Interpretation*. New York: Holt.

Allport, G. W. and Vernon, P. E. (1933). *Studies in Expressive Movement*. New York: Macmillan.

Alschuler, R. H. and Hattwick, L. W. (1947). *Painting and Personality*. Chicago: University of Chicago Press.

Aronoff, N. and McCormick, N. (1990). Psychodiagnostic processes: Projective techniques, sex, sex role identification and college students' projective drawings. *Journal of Clinical Psychology*, 46(4), pp. 460–466.

Aronson, E. (1958). 'The need for achievement as measured by graphic expression', in Atkinson, J. W. (ed.), *Motives in Fantasy, Action and Society*. Princeton: Von Nostrand Press, pp. 249–265.

Bieliaskas, V. J. (1960). Sexual identification in children's drawings of the human figure. *Journal of Clinical Psychology*, 16, 42–44.

Brick, M. (1944). Mental hygiene value of children's art work. *American Journal of Orthopsychiatry*, 14, pp. 136–148.

Brown, D. G. and Tolor, A. (1957). Human figure drawings as indicators of sexual identification and inversion. *Perceptual Motor Skills*, 7, pp. 199.

Buchanan, R. (1995). 'Rhetoric, humanism and design', in Buchanan, R. and Margolin, V. (eds.), *Discovering Design*. Chicago: University of Chicago Press, pp. 23–68.

Buck, J. N. (1950). Richmond Proceedings (mimeographed copy). California: Western Psychological Services. (Quoted in Hammer, 1980).

Burt, R. B. (1968). *An Exploratory Study of Personality Manifestations in Paintings*. Doctoral dissertation, Duke University (Dissertation Abstracts International 29, 1493–B Order number 68–14, 298).

Cox, M. V. (1993). *Children's Drawings of the Human Figure*. Hove: Lawrence Erlbaum.

Elkich, P. (1945). *Children's Drawings in a Projective Technique*. Psychological Monographs, vol. 58. Evanston, IL: American Psychological Association.

Fancher, R. E. (1979). *Pioneers of Psychology*. New York: W.W. Norton.

Hammer, E. F. (1980). *The Clinical Application of Projective Drawings*. Springfield: Charles C. Thomas.

Jolles, I. (1952). A study of the validity of some hypotheses for the qualitative interpretation of the H-T-P for children of elementary school age I sexual identification. *Journal of Clinical Psychology*, 8, 113–118.

Knop, I. and Richards, T.W. (1952). The children's differentiation of sex as reflected in drawings of the human figure. *Journal of Genetic Psychology*, 81, 99–112.

Koch, S. and Leary, D. (eds.). (1992). *A Century of Psychology as Science*. Washington, DC: American Psychological Association.

Krout, J. (1950). Symbol elaboration test. *Psychological Monographs, AMA*, 4, pp. 404–405.

Little, K. B. and Schneidman, E. S. (1955). The validity of thematic projective technique interpretations. *Journal of Personality*, 23, pp. 285–294.

Mainord, F. B. (1953). A note on the use of figure drawings in the diagnosis of sexual inversion. *Journal of Clinical Psychology*, 9, pp. 188–189.

Matthews, C., Hill, C., Case, F. and Allisma, T. (2010). Personal bias: The influence of personality profile on residential design decisions. *Housing and Society*, 37(1), pp. 1–24.

Papadakis-Michaelides, E. A. (1989). *Development of Children's Drawings in Relation to Gender and Culture*. Unpublished doctoral thesis, University of Birmingham, UK.

Precker, J. (1950). Painting and drawing in personality assessment: Summary. *Journal of Projective Techniques*, 14, pp. 262–286.

Read, H. (1953). *Art and Industry*. London: Faber and Faber.

Read, H. (1958). *Education through Art*. London: Faber and Faber.

Rogoff, I. (1998). 'Studying visual culture', in Mirzoeff, N. (ed.), *The Visual Culture Reader*. London: Routledge, pp. 14–26.

Roy, R. and Wield, D. (1989). *Product Design and Technological Innovation*. Philadelphia: Open University, Taylor and Francis.

Sudjic, D. (2009). *The Language of Things*. London: Penguin.

Tolor, A. and Tolor, B. (1955). The judgement of children's popularity from their human figure drawings. *Journal of Projective Techniques*, 19, pp. 170–176.

Tolor, A. and Tolor, B. (1974). Children's figure drawings and changing attitudes towards sex roles. *Psychological Reports*, 34, pp. 343–349.

Waehner, T. S. (1946). Interpretations of spontaneous drawings and paintings. *Genetic Psychology Monograph*, 33, pp. 3–70.

Weider, A. and Noller, P. A. (1953). Objective studies of children's drawings of human figures. II. Sex, age, intelligence. *Journal of Clinical Psychology*, 9, pp. 20–23.

Wolff, W. (1948). *Diagrams of the Unconscious*. New York: Grune and Stratton.

Zimmerman, J. and Garfinkle, L. (1942). Preliminary study of the art productions of the adult psychotic. *Psychiatric Quarterly*, 16, pp. 313–318.

Chapter 3

Inferring personality from drawings

Bill Wylie

Graphic expression

'Imagination' connects you at once with aesthetic activity and with language. It refers directly to images which Jung describes as the main content of the unconscious (Hillman, 1983, p. 32). Thinking, feeling and acting are requisites for self-expression, and people's graphic expression offers insights into aspects of people's being. An understanding of the ways a graphic expression can mirror aspects of the person producing it may offer important insights into brand creatives insofar as the graphic expression they initiate or are involved with may unwittingly emit messages that may be picked up at some level by consumers. There is a literature that suggests that consumers, in selecting between products, are seeking products that match their self-concept (Brock, 1965; Crozier and Greenhalgh, 1992; Hammer, 1995; Karande et al., 1997; De Chernatony et al., 2004). An understanding of the concepts unwittingly conveyed by graphic expression is a relevant analytical tool in ascertaining whether the concepts conveyed by a product match or mirror those of the consumers.

If a person is not in harmony, then there will be inhibition in one or other aspects of his or her self-expression. Such inhibition may be described as a blockage in the natural flow of harmonious being. The result is a dysfunction of communication either externally with society or internally with the whole self and, as Cordess has stated, 'There is increasing evidence that disorders of personality are associated with personal histories of failed attachment, neglect and frequently physical and sexual abuse. They are developmental disorders of the integrity of self, of self-awareness and of sympathy for others' (Cordess, 1997, p. 114). It has been observed that the population of HMP Grendon is characterised by high levels of personality disorder, psychiatric symptomatology, significant loss or separation from parental figures and incidence of physical and/or sexual abuse (Shine and Newton, 2000).

Genders and Player (1995) defined the therapeutic community (TC) regime at Grendon as one which incorporates a strong behavioural component, whereby an individual's actions are examined with surgical precision and commented on by the whole community. It entails the detailed and comprehensive assessment and analysis of behavioural patterns, wherein as much significance is granted to the questions of where and when the problem arises, and what maintains it, as is accorded to the questions that have preoccupied the psychoanalytic school of why the problem exists and how it has come into being. This frees the individual from automatically, and largely unconsciously, following entrenched modes of thought and action, and enables him to make choices about his future conduct so that ineffective or problematic patterns of behaviour can be avoided, and an alternative and more satisfying lifestyle adopted.

Equally importantly, however, engaging in therapeutic activities as a member of a TC also involves participation in mutual and reciprocal relationships with other members. Hence, in addition to furnishing a vivid setting in which problems may be explored and treated, the community affords a climate in which feelings of isolation and alienation can be dissipated, and a sense of belonging engendered. The TC, therefore, is designed to operate at the outer supportive levels, as well as the deeper exploratory levels, of psychotherapy. In such a setting, therapeutic treatment focuses on offence-paralleling behaviour and reducing risk of future offending. The therapy is directed towards the achievement of insight and a greater level of self-awareness. Research evidence has indicated that certain factors showed a high correlation with the risk of future recidivism, and these criminogenic factors are affected by the concept of multifactorial therapy supported by a multidisciplinary team (Shine and Morris, 2000, p. 202): 'The significance of this milieu is in understanding the functioning of the multidisciplinary team and contributions made from the different therapeutic paradigms.' Art therapy provides a significant contribution to this holistic process. By formally describing, analysing and evaluating the work carried out on the Assessment Unit at HMP Grendon, this research clarifies the value of using art therapy as a contribution to the assessment of suitability for TC engagement.

Art therapy

Waller and Dalley (1992) suggest that art therapy is a term that has been used to describe a collection of diverse practices held together fundamentally by their practitioners' belief in the healing value of image making. The focus of art therapy is the image, and the process involves a transaction between the maker, the artefact and the therapist. As in all therapies, bringing unconscious feelings to consciousness and thereafter exploring them hold true of art therapy, but here the richness of artistic symbol and metaphor illuminates the process.

According to the British Association of Art Therapists, art therapy is a form of therapy in which the making of visual images – paintings, drawings and so forth – in the presence of a qualified art therapist contributes towards externalisation of thoughts and feelings that may otherwise remain unexpressed. The images may have a diagnostic as well as a therapeutic function in that they provide the individual and the therapist with a visible record of the session and give indicators for further treatment. Art therapists may work with the transference – that is the feelings from the past that are projected onto the therapist in the session. Such feelings are usually contained by the artwork, and this enables resolution to take place indirectly if necessary (British Association of Art Therapists, 1989).

Grendon's purpose as a TC is to increase individual confidence and self-esteem, to reduce offending tendencies and to develop more positive relationships with others. Therapy contributes to the milieu by encouraging pro-social behaviour in the context of a complementary group process; therein is the possibility for creatively addressing and promoting such qualities as empathy and communication skills, listening to others, appropriate expression of emotions and awareness of one's own behaviour. According to Schaverien (1987, p. 84),

> Once an image exists 'out there', in the world, it interacts with and affects the artist. It also interacts with and affects other people, the consequences of which have repercussions for the artist. For the client in therapy, who is unable to relate easily to other

people, who is also perhaps unable to relate to herself, the image-making process may play a fundamental part in enabling her to begin to do so. To make something that can be seen can authenticate her experience and even her existence.

Creativity is a process of perception, the interaction of unconscious and conscious modes of thinking. The art therapist is involved with creative expression and making visual equivalents for inner feelings. This is a psychodynamic process that facilitates self-awareness through reflection on the imagery produced, thus influencing behaviour and social functioning. By this process, the self is externalised; communicated through creativity, emotion is viewed in imagery, interpreted and acknowledged. 'Play, and the use of art forms, and religious practice, tend in various but allied ways towards a unification and integration of the personality. For instance, play can easily be seen to link the individual's relation to external reality' (Winnicott, 1964, p. 145). Winnicott believed that psychoanalysis was a specialised form of play, and that part of the therapist's remit is the facilitation of such activity for children and adults. Art therapy is an exploratory process that enables the individual to reflect upon the past and its influence on the present and on the future. The artwork encourages the maker to engage with his or her true thoughts and feelings. For instance, personality disorders are ingrained and enduring behaviour patterns; reflecting on past history through image making develops awareness of the person's responses to life experience, while the images facilitate acknowledgement of the individual's emotional reaction to events, thereby promoting the potential for change. In execution and content, the picture reveals evidence of the true person rather than how the person chooses to present or see him- or herself. As such, art therapy is a unique psychotherapeutic service providing support for improvement with coping skills and in the long term contributes to personal and social integration.

In a paper exploring the role of the case study in art therapy research, Edwards has stated, 'Image-making, story-telling, therapy and research are each, in their way, concerned with joining together actions, intentions, emotions, perceptions and events into meaningful narratives, though these narratives may take different forms' (Edwards, 1999, p. 7). The picture produced in art therapy is a story of a person in time, a history of experience, a narration of the person's passage through life with ethical connotations – it is a visual expression of meaning, for the image has intention. Therefore, it is possible to compare the construction of intention composed by different individuals under similar circumstances.

A number of features are taken into account. The structure of representation is educative in that the picture created by one individual may be compared to the image produced by another person in the same setting. Where colour is concerned, in a study designed to assess the impact of drawing topic on children's colour use when drawing affectively salient topics, it was concluded that children tend to associate a negative emotion with dark colours – for example black or brown – while yellow and orange are often associated with positive happy feelings (Burkitt and Newell, 2005). Additionally, where size is concerned, it has been observed that children depict the emotional significance of a drawn topic through size, whereby appealing figures are exaggerated in size and potentially threatening figures are reduced in size (Thomas et al., 1989).

Moreover, in visual terms, temporal symbolism is present in an artwork such that the picture can be read from left to right, from past to future with the present centrally placed (see Buck and Warren, 1995, for further reference to temporal placement). The image provides an indication of the psychological propensity of the maker and as Buck and Warren have observed, 'The proportion, perspective, and details in a drawing are general characteristics that can provide information about the functioning of an individual in the context of their expected level of functioning' (Buck and Warren, 1995, p. 25).

It is submitted here that these conclusions regarding colour and size are as pertinent in the consideration of artwork made by adults who do not have the experience of art education. With reference to the initial stage of working with the art therapy process, Case (1998) concluded that in an assessment, there are the twin tasks of discovering if the person is able to make use of a therapeutic space, as well as assessing the person's state of mind in terms of his or her inner world and the effect of the outer environment upon him or her.

Rationale of present research

The present research is designed to define aspects of image making that might be used to assess readiness to engage in treatment – that is the TC model of therapy. This treatment is highly demanding emotionally, intellectually and socially, requiring motivation and readiness to engage. A quantitative research paradigm was employed in which images produced by respondents were rated across seven scales. This process was informed by psychoanalytic theory and the literature on interpretation of images in art therapy. Therefore, the research lays the foundation for further quantitative research to demonstrate the extent to which predictions of readiness for treatment based on these elements are accurate.

Methodology

Primary data were collated from ten subjects over the period from March 2004 to May 2005. All artwork was created by participants in the Assessment Unit and made during a two-hour experiential session of art therapy provided for new admissions to HMP Grendon.

At the beginning of the session, the art therapy process was described and a theme for image making was offered that contained an element of choice to the group. The men were asked to consider their reasons for coming to Grendon with reference to their past lives and their hopes for the future. Additionally, they might use the session as an opportunity to express what they were feeling at that particular moment. In other words, participants were asked to think about their lives and express that engagement in visual equivalents. No suggestions or specific directives are given as to the placement of elements within the compositional structure.

Once collected, the artwork was rated using a pre-established rating scale consisting of seven elements. All were amenable to objective assessment, and since seven scales were used, each attracting up to a maximum of ten points per scale, each individual piece of artwork could attract a total of between 0 and 70 points. A judgement was made that scores of 35 and above indicated a temperament that was suitable for group work, whereas scores of less than 35 were indicative of a temperament that would not respond well to group work. The seven rating scales used were as follows:

1   Use of space – utilisation of surface area of the paper – for example whether all three parts of the page are employed; a small drawing relative to the size of paper is indicative of inhibition or unwillingness to participate.
2   Use of colour – the addition of colour indicates emotional investment.
3   Use of diverse art materials – the greater the use of diverse materials, the greater involvement and desire for clarity in communication are indicated.

4 Realistic composition – the extent to which there is realism in the drawing; this indicates the capacity for reality confrontation.

5 Temporal symbolism – whether the image is structured to be read from left to right, from past to future.

6 Maturity of representation – the more mature the representation is, the more it indicates the presence of cognitive resources.

7 Theme – whether the same prominence is given to all the three parts of the theme on the page; the extent to which this is followed shows the ability to persist with a single theme.

The overall rating figure produced was subsequently compared with the external measures to establish the extent to which they correlated. There were three external measures: (1) whether those men allocated to a therapy wing remained there; (2) whether those men allocated to a therapy wing left without completing therapy; and (3) whether men were not allocated to a therapy wing at all. It was predicted that the men falling into category (1) would achieve a score of 35 or above, while men falling into categories (2) and (3) would achieve scores of less than 35.

In addition to the overall rating figure, session notes were kept, analysing the conscious and unconscious symbolism of the images produced. These art therapy assessments were, however, made independently of contributions made by other members of the staff. At a later stage, the resulting analysis was compared with the summaries of assessment contributed by the other members of the multidisciplinary team – for example psychometric testing that included Raven's Standard Progressive Matrices, Eysenck's Personality Questionnaire and Blame Attribution Inventory, as well as included psychology and probation reports addressing psychopathy, risk assessment and cognitive function. Consideration of these characteristics provides further evidence of subjects' motivational and emotional/ intellectual capacity to engage with an intensive psychological treatment programme.

Results

According to this analysis, six of the ten subjects produced artwork that attracted less than 35 points, while five subjects produced work that attracted 35 points or more. The summation of the scores produced total scores of 9, 12, 16, 20, 24, 36, 40, 41, 56 and 58. In this way, five subjects were deemed unsuitable, and five suitable, for group work. In actual fact, six respondents (those with the six lowest marks) whose work was deemed unsuitable left the prison within a year of the assessment, whereas the four subjects with marks easily over the 35-point limit, deemed to be suitable for group work, are still at the prison after three years. Since decisions about the respondents were made in isolation from the art therapeutic assessments, and since remaining at the prison is a sign of suitability for group work (the main function of the prison), the art therapeutic assessments showed high levels of validity.

Discussion

In a paper exploring the role of the case study in art therapy research, Edwards has stated, 'Image-making, story-telling, therapy and research are each, in their way, concerned with joining together actions, intentions, emotions, perceptions and events into meaningful narratives, though these narratives may take different forms' (1999, p. 7). Men on the Assessment Unit often choose black paper to symbolise their unhappy past or used bright colours, especially yellow, to represent a positive hope for the future. A negative approach is described ahead in example 2, where the participant produced a small drawing relating to an unhappy event.

As stated, many participants in the experiential session of art therapy on the Assessment Unit at Grendon chose to engage with all three aspects of their lives – past, present and future. It is further observed that in visual terms, this temporal symbolism is constructed in such a manner that the picture can be read from left to right, from past to future, with the present centrally placed. A number of examples are described here in detail to illustrate these principles. We will begin with examples that point to individuals who would respond positively to therapeutic work. This is followed by examples from individuals whose work reveals an opposite tendency.

Example 1 (Figure 3.1) is a drawing made by a man who had difficulty with emotional expression but who persisted in his endeavour to visually describe aspects of his life. He sat for some time before starting to draw. He could not think of a satisfactory image to describe his past or future, and so he concentrated on the present that he described as 'going through a tunnel with a light at the other end'. This was in reference to his coming to Grendon with the hope that therapy would help him to change. The centrally placed image of a rail track going through a dark tunnel inspired him to talk about his past; remembering childhood holidays by the seaside, he began to draw sandcastles to the left of the central, 'present' metaphor. In the area below the sandcastles, there was a weapon and as he drew, he related the reason for his imprisonment. Becoming more relaxed, the participant was able to imagine a future that he hoped would be tranquil and peaceful. To the right of the tunnel, he drew mountains and a lake that encapsulated his hopes for the future. The participant had been anxious and uncommunicative at the beginning of the session, reticent to reveal himself. By the end of the session, however, he had become more relaxed and communicative. This man had been in the army and then in prison, environments where control over the self is of primary importance, where emotional expression is unacceptable. Yet within a single session of two-hour duration, he had revealed much about his life experience and had expressed feelings regarding these experiences.

Moreover, further examination of the picture reveals the extent to which the subject is able to address the three periods of his life – the past, the present and the future – thereby exhibiting a capacity to engage with all three aspects, and he was able to discuss them in a social context. The structure of the imagery is such that the journey of his life could be read from left to right – the past was drawn on the left, the present was centrally placed and the future was on the right. It is suggested that this narrative movement, the telling of a story and consequent reading of it from left to right, is indicative of someone who has a capacity to participate in therapeutic process. That he has a willingness to attend to all three aspects of his life with the intention to change is evident from the placement of the three chronological periods, starting with the past, moving to the right across the paper and concluding with a symbol for the future. In this example, the movement towards the future is emphasised by the rail track, which curves to the right, through a dark tunnel to the light of future, peace and tranquillity. The change of affect from inhibited unease to open self-expression communicated the man's ability to become involved with therapy.

There are three other examples of artwork pointing to suitability to engage in group therapy. The first, as shown in the original, introduces colour into the upper left quadrant, addressing early emotional experience (Figure 3.2). The second uses colour to emphasise meaning – the picture is divided into half, with the left section coloured black (negative past) in contrast to the

Figure 3.1 Positive image.

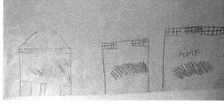

Figure 3.2 Positive image.

Figure 3.3 Positive image.

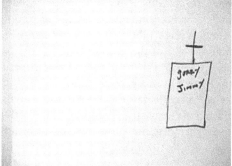

Figure 3.4 Negative image.

right section, which is coloured yellow (positive future) (Figure 3.3). Finally, there are examples 4–6 showing willingness to participate, expressed by making three separate images and by using diverse art materials (Figures 3.4–3.6).

In terms of examples of artwork pointing to unsuitability to engage in the therapeutic group work, the first is example 7 (Figure 3.4), a drawing of a man who was deemed unsuited for group therapy at the time of attending the art therapy session. He too had difficulty with emotional expression, seemed anxious with the situation and was reticent to communicate. The outcome of the session was, however, quite different to the previous example. After sitting motionless for some time, the man decided to fold his paper in half, an indication that he was unwilling to address the 'enormity' of the task placed before him – that is he was unable to openly express his feelings by using the whole of the paper. Again, this area of paper was too great for he drew a tiny gravestone to the right of centre, an image insignificant in proportion to the potential area available for the construction of a picture. Nothing more was added. Yet this small revelation had been too great, for he put down his pencil, rose and left the room. He remained in Grendon for just four months.

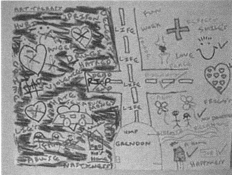

Figure 3.5 Positive image.

Figure 3.6 Positive image.

It is concluded that example 7, the drawing of a gravestone, showed evidence of someone who was unsuitable for therapy at that time. The man folded his paper in half, thereby indicating restraint, an unwillingness to openly express himself. Reticence to communicate emotion was symbolised by the difficulty he experienced with starting to draw, then by the minimal size of the object placed on the paper to the right of centre. This placement was also unusual in that the subject matter relating to a past event was positioned to the right in the area normally reserved for illustrating the future. The gravestone was surrounded by empty space; it was without context, again showing inability to address the subject. Finally, the need to leave the room was an indication that the man was not suitable for therapy.

Further negative examples, showing unsuitability for group therapy, are provided by examples 8–10. Example 8 demonstrates the non-use of space, save for the 'confining' house in the top-left quadrant representative of the past. The subject was unable to engage further and threw the image into a rubbish bin (Figure 3.10). Within three months of arrival at Grendon, the man left, showing his unsuitability for therapy. Then comes example 9. This image presents simplistic constructions indicating that the subject would be intellectually challenged by the rigours of therapeutic process (Figure 3.7). Finally, there is example 10, with a theme and composition indicating fantasy, betokening the inability to engage with immediate reality. The future is represented by a spacecraft 'escaping' from the Earth and moving in a direction betokening the past (Figure 3.8).

It can be seen from these examples how artwork can assist in the assessment of a capacity to engage with therapy or not, as the case might be. The themes addressed the construction or composition of the picture and the participant's behaviour and interaction with others; all contribute to the assessment. Space does not permit description of further comparison of artworks that take account of the stated considerations plus the emotive use of colour. The two images described were monochrome drawings; the positive image was a pencil drawing and the negative one made use of a black felt-tip pen, both on white paper.

As stated earlier, the image is a symbol of the maker's experience of being in the world, and the degree to which he engages with the image-making process is an indication of his capacity for further engagement in group work. The first illustration was a positive example of someone who was willing to enter a therapeutic alliance through visual expression. He did this by imaginatively conveying a desire to address the totality of his life; the past, present

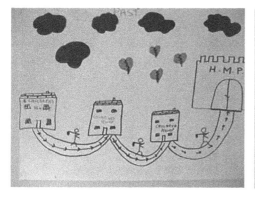

Figure 3.7 Negative image.

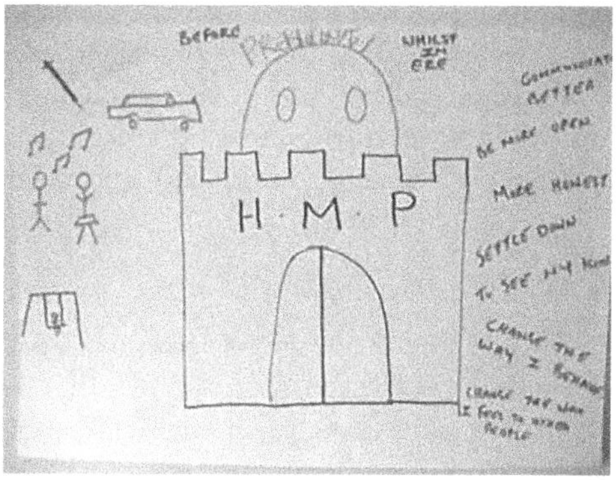

Figure 3.8 Negative image.

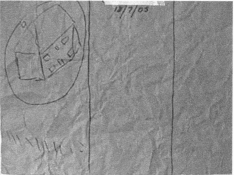

Figure 3.9 Positive image.

Figure 3.10 Negative image.

and future were graphically communicated in chronological sequence across the paper from left to right, from past to future. I would, however, argue that the lack of colour indicates a degree of emotional reserve, as the artist John Constable wrote, 'painting is with me but another word for feeling' (Gombrich, 1987, p. 234). Moreover, in his book on art and psychoanalysis, Fuller described aesthetics as 'the specific structuring of feeling' (Fuller, 1980, p. 187), and in considering the image-making process as a depiction of the outside world and expression of the internal world of the maker, he has identified an underlying biological influence on aesthetics that can be defined in terms of object relations theory or the concept of fusion and separation related to child development. Space does not permit a detailed investigation of this comparison; suffice to say that Fuller refers to Milner's book *On Not Being Able to Paint* (ibid., p. 142), in which the analyst described her attempt to find visual equivalence to her psychological/emotional experiences. She noted that when painting, there occurred 'a fusion into a never-before-known wholeness: not only were the object and oneself no longer felt to be separate but neither were thought and sensation and feeling and action' (ibid., p. 143). This led her to suggest that the sense of union achieved in attempts to create a work of art, 'this transcendence of separateness, might it not have its parallel in the union with other people that working together for a common purpose achieves?' (Milner, 1950, p. 143). For Milner, there was a fear to be encountered in the abandonment to colour, a fear of what might happen if one let go of one's mental hold on the drawn outline that kept everything in its place – the outline represented the world of facts. I would suggest that in addition to representing external reality, drawing facilitates a definition of reality, and this expression is more clearly enhanced by the use of colour.

Conclusion

'In broadening the range of perceptual experiences and exercising imagination one's mind doesn't simply change; it grows. It grows not only because of the variety, but also through deepening and sharing experiences' (Feagin and Maynard, 1997, p. 3). By formally describing, analysing and evaluating the work currently carried out on the Assessment Unit at Grendon TC Prison, it is the aim of this research to clarify the value of using art therapy as a contribution to the assessing of the suitability of an individual for TC engagement. The manner in which the image is executed is an expressive representation of the individual's state of being. In other words, the style and content of the artwork reflect the psychic state of the person and as such can provide evidence for the suitability of the person to engage further in therapy. Therefore, the imagery produced on admittance to the Assessment Unit, in addition to affect, provides relevant information about individual attitude towards participation in this therapeutic environment, and thus can be influential in helping to determine: (a) overall suitability for group therapy and (b) length of stay on the assessment wing prior to a move onto a main wing of the prison, or return to sending establishment.

In the course of analysing an artwork from an art therapy perspective, it can be seen how unconsciously visuals associated with products could also give off images and personalities. Given the importance of the mirroring principle (Brock, 1965; Crozier and Greenhalgh, 1992; Hammer, 1995; Karande et al., 1997; De Chernatony et al., 2004) and the need to ensure that products match the self-concept of customers, it is important to understand the images that might be given off by a product. Only then can an assessment be made of whether the product is likely to match the customer's self-image.

References

British Association of Art Therapists. (1989). *Artists and Arts Therapists: A Brief Discussion of their Roles within Hospitals, Clinics, Special Schools and in the Community.* Standing Committee of Arts Therapists, Brighton.

Brock, T. C. (1965). Communicator – recipient similarity and decision change. *Journal of Personality and Social Psychology*, 1, pp. 650–654.

Buck, J. N. and Warren, W. L. (1995). *House-Tree-Person. Projective Drawing Technique.* Manual and Interpretive Guide, Los Angeles, CA, Western Psychological Services.

Burkitt, E. and Newell, T. (2005). Effects of human figure on children's use of colour to depict sadness and happiness. *International Journal of Art Therapy*, 10(1), pp. 15–22.

Case, C. (1998). Brief encounters: Thinking about images in assessment. *Inscape, the Journal of the British Association of Art Therapists*, 3(1), pp. 26–33.

Cordess, C. (1997). Our responsibilities as forensic psychotherapists. *Rampton Hospital Research News*, p. 114.

Crozier, W. and Greenhalgh, P. (1992). The empathy principle: Towards a model for the psychology of art. *Journal for the Theory of Social Behaviour*, 22, pp. 63–79.

De Chernatony, L., Drury, S. and Segal-Horn, S. (2004). Identifying and sustaining services brands values. *Journal of Marketing Communications*, 10, pp. 73–94.

Edwards, D. (1999). The role of the case study in art therapy research. *Inscape, the Journal of the British Association of Art Therapists*, 4(1), pp. 2–9.

Feagin, S. L. and Maynard, P. (eds.). (1997). *Aesthetics*. Oxford University Press, Oxford.

Fuller, P. (1980). *Art and Psychoanalysis*. Writers & Readers Publishing Co-operative, London.

Genders, E. and Player, E. (1995). *Grendon: A Study of a Therapeutic Prison*. Clarendon Press, Oxford.

Gombrich, E. H. (1987). *Art and Illusion*, 5th edn. Phaidon Press, London, p. 324.

Hammer, M. (1995). *Reengineering the Corporation*. Nicholas Brealey, London.

Hillman, J. (1983). *Inter Views*. Harper and Row, New York.

Karande, K., Zinkhan, G. M. and Lum, A. B. (1997). Brand personality and self concept: A replication and extension. *American Marketing Association Summer Conference*, 8, pp. 165–171.

Milner, M. (1950). *On Not Being Able to Paint*. Heineman, London.

Schaverien, J. (1987). The scapegoat and the talisman: Transference in art therapy. In: T. Dalley, C. Case, J. Schavenen, F. Weir, D. Halliday, P. Nowell Hall, and D. Waller (eds.), *Images of Art Therapy: New Developments in Theory and Practice*. Tavistock, London, pp. 84–85.

Shine, J. and Morris, M. (2000). Addressing criminogenic needs in a prison therapeutic community. Association of Therapeutic communities *Therapeutic Communities*, 21(3), pp. 197–219.

Shine, J. and Newton, M. (2000). Damaged, disturbed and dangerous: A profile of receptions to Grendon therapeutic prison 1995–2000. In: J. Shine (ed.), *A Compilation of Grendon Research*. Leyhill Press, Grendon, pp. 23–35.

Thomas, G. V., Chaigne, E. and Fox, T. J. (1989). Children's drawings of topics differing in significance: Effects on size of drawing. *British Journal of Developmental Psychology*, 7, pp. 321–331.

Waller, D. and Dalley, T. (1992). Art therapy: A theoretical perspective. In: D. Waller and A. Gilroy (eds.), *Art Therapy: A Handbook*. Open University Press, Buckingham, pp. 3–24.

Winnicott, D. W. (1964). *The Child, the Family and the Outside World*. Penguin Press, Harmondsworth.

Chapter 4

Personality as reflected in creatives' adverts

Jim Blythe

Advertising creative are at the sharp end of creativity. The people who design and develop new advertising (the so-called creatives) are usually talented artists, musicians or wordsmiths who have found a commercial outlet for their talents – it has been said that advertising copywriters would sell their souls for a potted message: the ability to convey a message in a few words, a single image or a few bars of music is at the root of all advertising success.

Of course, the artistry is constrained by the client. Advertising creatives are given a brief, from which they need to develop a rough outline of what they intend to do: the client then approves the rough (or not) and the work either goes ahead to a full treatment or is adapted to suit the client's needs. This is the area in which the creatives sometimes become bogged down because they then find that their creative urges are curbed by the client's wish to do something incremental – that is something which follows on from previous advertising and which is therefore not seen as being as original as the creatives might have liked it to be. The need to present solutions that the client will like therefore presents a potential obstacle to the achievement of diverse, creative solutions.

This chapter builds on research carried out with advertising creatives in London. The research was carried out using a grounded theory approach involving an in-depth analysis of qualitative data: because this approach is perhaps less well-known to many readers, some explanation of the methodology is probably in order.

Methodology

The grounded theory approach to research operates under an interpretivist paradigm. The intention is to generate theory rather than arrive at an objective truth. In the words of Corbin and Strauss (1990, p. 4),

> Grounded theorists share a conviction with many other qualitative researchers that the usual canons of 'good science' should be retained, but require redefinition in order to fit in the realities of qualitative research and the complexities of social phenomena . . . significance, theory-observation compatibility, generalisability, consistency, reproducibility, precision and verification.

Grounded theory follows a set of ten procedures, but (by its nature) the procedures are not necessarily followed in strict order, and several iterations of a given procedure might be needed before the researcher moves onto the next phase of the research. The activities involved are summarised in Table 4.1.

Table 4.1 The processes of a grounded theory study.

Activity	Description
Collect data	Semi-structured interviews and observation are most commonly used, but any textual data may be used.
Transcribe data	A full transcript of the interview or other data is made.
Develop categories	Open coding of the transcripts is used to categorise comments.
Saturate categories	The data is analysed according to the categories developed, the researcher proceeding through the transcripts as often as is necessary until all the examples of comments in each category have been gathered.
Abstract definitions	Formal definitions of the categories are developed by reference to the data gathered.
Theoretical sampling	Relevant samples of comments are abstracted with the aim of testing and developing the categories further.
Axial coding	The development of relationships between the categories.
Theoretical integration	A core category is identified around which the other categories are linked to existing theory.
Grounding the theory	The emergent theory is grounded by returning to the data and validating it against actual segments of text.
Filling in gaps	Further collection of data to fill in any missing detail.

Source: Adapted from Bartlett and Payne (1997).

Part of the problem with using a grounded theory approach is that it relies on the establishment on the part of the researcher of a long-term relationship with the data. Final results may easily take a long period to analyse; the research itself can never be considered to be 'finished'; and the interpretation of the data is necessarily subjective and requires considerable navel-gazing on the part of the researcher.

In common with other interpretivist methodologies, grounded theory does not pretend to arrive at an objective, generalisable truth: what it is intended to achieve is a development of theory, some of which is explained by a return to the literature.

Method

The research was conducted with eight advertising creatives and one branding consultant, all based in the London area. A breakfast meeting was convened, and the group was encouraged to talk about their experiences in creating and interpreting brand personalities. The discussion was initiated by asking each member of the group to say what kind of animal they most resembled personally, and how this had affected their approach to their creative work. As an approach, this started the conversation going, but was only partially successful in eliciting a direct response: interestingly, the five animals mentioned were the fox (because it is sly and is able to get its own way without giving anything away), the hyena (for similar reasons to the fox), the unicorn (because it is magical, colourful and mythical), the chameleon (because it is adaptable) and the bear (because it can appear large and friendly, but can also be aggressive).

The creatives were also asked to bring samples of their best work, a task which they interpreted as meaning samples of their favourite work. The intention in doing this was to

Table 4.2 Categories against which views were categorised.

Category	Description
Conflict vs. co-operation	This category is concerned with conflict between work colleagues (the other half of the team), much of which was regarded as positive. The conflicts largely arise as a result of personality differences, leading to creative solutions.
Sensitive vs. insensitive	At times creatives need to be sensitive in order to empathise with the target audience and with the marketers from the firm, but also need to be insensitive when their work is criticised.
Career vs. creation	Some creatives are career-orientated; others are more motivated by the impulse to create.
Passion vs. discipline	Becoming emotionally involved in the creative process is necessary, but also creatives need to be disciplined in order to produce finished work which meets the brief.
Creatives vs. agency	Some creatives are able to be 'company men' while others see themselves as 'free spirits'.

encourage discussion about the relationship between the personality of the individual and the communications the individual had produced.

Collecting and transcribing the data in a grounded theory study are a somewhat time-consuming task: fortunately, once the interview data has been transcribed, much of the remaining analysis can be assisted by the use of computers. Open coding of the transcripts led to the development of data categories: the initial reading of the transcript generated almost 30 possible categories, but these were amalgamated into a final five categories of data, which were defined as shown in Table 4.1.

The transcript was then re-examined, and the data divided up between these categories; several iterations of the process were needed in order to ensure that data was correctly attributed to the appropriate category. In some cases, respondents' statements could be considered under more than one category, but these cases were surprisingly few.

Given the way creatives work, there is a natural bias in favour of diversity: this naturally led to dichotomies and even to conflicts in the reported data. In the next section, we will see that conflict is not necessarily a bad thing as we expand on the elements in Table 4.2.

Conflict vs. co-operation

Broadly speaking, conflict is a psychosocial outcome of interaction (Ruekert and Walker, 1987) and can be described as a breakdown or disruption in normal activities in such a way that the individuals or groups concerned experience difficulty working together (Reitz, 1977; Hellreigel and Slocum, 1988; Hodge and Anthony, 1991; Hatch, 1997; Daft, 1998). Traditionally, conflict is viewed as being dysfunctional – in other words we tend to see conflict as a bad thing, as something that gets in the way of getting the job done. Conflict is often seen as impacting negatively on the organisation, reducing productivity and decreasing morale, because attention focuses on the conflict rather than on organisational aims.

However, conflict is inevitable where people have a diversity of backgrounds, interests and talents. In the case of advertising creatives, conflict is the sand in the oyster shell, creating an irritation that leads to original ideas. This is known as the interactions or functional view of conflict, and implies that conflict can be a positive force which helps effective performance and encourages creativity. Far from diverting attention away from the aims of the organisation, conflict ultimately generates more effective ways of achieving those aims.

Creatives usually work as part of a two-person team. This is a time-honoured system in advertising agencies, producing conflicts which lead to creative solutions. The creatives were clear about the importance of this type of relationship, as these quotes show:

> I think personalities get quite interesting as well when they're full of contradictions. You know, I think I know what he's going to say next and then he'll throw something in and it'll contradict . . .
>
> Keith did a lot of the work in terms of the concept, and the stuff that went out actually ended up being critical with them going through them but without Keith it wouldn't have worked. He would definitely call himself a bowler, and he needed a batsman. It's quite interesting, an interesting scenario.

The concept of the batsman and the bowler, on opposite sides but playing the same game, was mentioned on other occasions.

> I think that teams are brought together through experience, and what you've got to do out of that and sometimes that could be [. . .] who was a production person, a producer, a project manager, but those kind of definitions and those boundaries don't matter. I think personality depends on how you work together, as a group, that dynamic group.
>
> I think my best work has been done with other people. It may be possible to be an artist, to be an absolute artist, to have complete control of your work but even that's a bit unnatural . . . and you do want to do it all yourself, but you reach a point where you can't release it, you react with other people, otherwise you can't achieve it within the time frame.
>
> You also think that you're going to try to find either one, whatever you get, so if there isn't a conflict with you, in the brief they've given you, you need a partner who'll create that in order to get the best out of you.

There was no evidence in this category that the personalities of the team members were expected to have an effect on the outcome of cracking the brief – in other words there was no expectation that the creatives would try to impose their collective personality on the finished brand identity to any extent. This may be because of a feeling that the aim of the exercise is to crack the brief rather than be independently creative.

The brief is not necessarily what gets you; it's the idea you come up with to crack the brief that gets you.

Sensitive vs. insensitive

The mental anguish of being a creative came through strongly, especially in terms of having to put one's work up for criticism by outsiders. This is an area in which being different can be painful – the creatives had often felt that their natural propensity to be original and different had been met with some hostility, and they therefore found themselves creating defensive barriers against this kind of response.

> In advertising you have to be sensitive and insensitive at the same time. Eh???
>
> I think you're asked to wear your heart on your sleeve.
>
> You have to be very tenacious to make it happen. I had a friend who was a junior at [. . .] and they taught their marketing people not to respond, at all, in meetings. So you'd go, you'd turn into an animal, swoosh around, turn into a shell, hard work explodes, and there's . . . [puts on a blank expression] [laughter] It's the kind of behaviour you hate.
>
> People like to show their work, and you come up with the most original funny TV ad and you have to show it to the most cynical people in the world and you're expecting, you know, a barrel full of laughs and get half a titter, yeah, that's horrible.
>
> I think what else is interesting is that adverts will try and use every personality in the creative process. We are actually creating you know sometimes a piece of work – we can be quite precious about it, saying, it's my baby, and we are creating something and I think in terms of what we just said is that we give something hopefully arms and legs and something that can go and live and breathe and whether it's gone through an agency or whatever, hopefully there's enough kind of tools and bits to that thing that it can go off and continue to live.
>
> Producing new raw material . . . There's this huge melting pot of creative people, much bigger than the whole advertising industry, much hungrier than the advertising industry, earning less money, and there's this huge cultural creative beast that has the stage and TV and drama where the opportunities are for celebrity and all those things, a whole world which is kind of . . . glossier than advertising.

This was an area in which the creatives felt that the individual's personality was likely to have an effect on the brand personality. Partly this was due to the ability of a professional, sensitive creative to understand and add to the brand identity proposed by the client, and partly it was due to the affinity the creative's personality might have for the brand personality.

> I brought in a programme which was designed as a passport. Basically it took you into the London Eye and put on an arts festival, for G8, a celebration of Africa, but I thought why is it my favourite? I think probably it's not even the biggest or the best, but I really I had such passion for the fact that I really think we could make a difference to people's lives on it, and so we brought over African growers, and we thought that it was really important that they bought into it and that they, in their own way, got what we were trying to do, and you could see the difference it made to them, and in the context of the G8, and then each show has got basically a different passport.

There is clearly an issue here involving emotional labour which is defined as 'the management of feeling to create a publicly observable facial and bodily display [which] is sold for a wage and therefore has exchange value' (Hochschild, 2003, p. 7). In the original work on emotional labour, the emphasis was on low-paid service sector jobs where staff were compelled to smile and say, 'Have a nice day' to each customer. In the business-to-business context, emotional labour is no less important, but it operates in a somewhat different way: the creatives were expected to display enthusiasm, competence and passion when showing the client their work. This took a certain toll on their sensitive, artistic natures, and in the long run could have an effect on the degree to which they were prepared to be diverse in their work.

Career vs. creation

The relationship between career aspirations and diversity is not unique to advertising industry creatives but it is certainly an area in which the creative's personality is likely to play a role in developing the brand personality. Career and creativity are not always in conflict: in some cases, a particularly creative piece of work is rewarded by the industry, and this can lead in turn to lucrative contracts and job offers.

> But for me, when I was young and creative, I was working to win an award a lot of the time . . . It was probably, I went too far that way, I wanted the glory, I wanted to be on the podium, and that's the basis . . .
>
> I've changed a bit in the interim, I don't think awards add much, they're still great. I don't think you can base a career on going out for awards, these days it's not as true that I feel like that. Probably because I haven't got any!
>
> In big agencies, the highest accolade you can win in advertising is the D&AD Black Pencil, and it actually guarantees you a job for the next ten years.
>
> You know if it's somewhere like [well-known agency], which has got a bit of name as, like, the song and dance agency, very successful in what they do, with the Halifax, with Johnny Ball, with whatever his name is, you would think of that as a great place to work, it's very, very successful mainstream advertising, I can't do that sort of stuff. You could put me in there and pay me £150,000, £450,000 a year, and I couldn't do it.
>
> That mainstream stuff is not going to win awards. You stay outside of that, on the margins, doing something different that hasn't been done before, they know that stuff like that, there isn't, at the end of it.

The issue coming out here is that the creative is likely to choose to work in an area that suits his or her personality – either in an environment where career is important or in one in which creativity is important.

The view was expressed that producing a creative, original piece of work was not necessarily the way to please the client: clients and agencies almost seem to operate with a bias against diversity.

> If you genuinely want to produce bags of work you have to be pretty sly about it. I don't think most people want genuine creative work. I think most people want progress from the thing they had before . . . So I would say, having said that, I would say I'm a fox.

This respondent admits to being like a fox in personality, but the next respondent talked about being more like a chameleon. The reference to paedophiles comes from an example provided by the interviewer, suggesting that creating a campaign for greater understanding of paedophiles would be a real challenge to the creatives.

> I think that's the best thing about this business, it's like a chameleon, you try and fit in somebody else's shoes and you can be the other guy, and you can probably get to understand the

paedophile, the intellectual one, what it would be like, so being aware that it wouldn't stick, that would be terrible but you could probably get to close enough, and go to the uncomfort zone, get to the discomfort zone, where you start thinking about it from that point of view, and so you do a job that other people couldn't possibly do.

For this respondent, the key to creativity was the challenge: trying to understand paedophiles without actually becoming one. (The interviewer offered an alternative scenario, that of being asked to develop a campaign for golfing equipment if one were a keen golfer. This was generally regarded as being much less interesting.) The overall implication of this part of the research was that creatives enjoy and embrace diversity, whereas clients and agencies tend to shy away from it.

Passion vs. discipline

Becoming passionate about cracking the brief while at the same time retaining the necessary professional detachment to carry out the task was another area the creatives regarded as a personality issue.

Passion's useless if you can't focus, if you can't discipline yourself. Unless you can focus that, that thing you've got, that spark . . .
Of course you use that inspirational force to get a lot of other people going.
The most important is you should get the passion to support the work.
Part of the passion is the challenging brief: challenges are often about avoiding the obvious.
It goes back to when I was working in an agency, they'd say, 'Oh, it's a tampon brief, let's get the girls in on that,' and we'd go like, no, a lot of great ads are in those sort of ways buzzing.
In reality it's all about challenge, you don't have like months off to celebrate – you're into the other job that's fallen by the wayside or picking up the next thing.
What you mean by that, going back to your example of the golf balls or the paedophile, to be honest you'd probably want the paedophile brief because you'd know that would be challenging.

In other words, passion is necessary but not sufficient – creatives also need to stay focused and remember that, as soon as one job finishes, another one will follow on.

Creatives vs. agency

It is in the area of relationships between the creatives and the agency (and hence the client) that one would expect the greatest impact on the brand personality. Creatives tend to have an uneasy relationship with those who set the brief, whether this is done by the client, by a branding agency or in-house. This often results in attempts to circumvent the agency in some way, or outwit it.

When you go in as a creative and try to do something more from the thing you're doing that's the thing . . . I don't think the money would be there, you want the reward of the commission, seeing something made, and feeling that, that you know your heart's in it and all of that, which is the kind of thing you need, has been you need an opportunity to nail the job to the ground – you know the commercial reality here is I don't think there are really that many opportunities to be creative unless you really want to smash something. Not an appealing prospect for most people who have to work with you or work within the confines of . . . So there's always the challenge. So I would say, having said that, having said that, I would say I'm a fox.

It's funny, something we've been going through for the past few weeks, I had a brief I had no idea what the branding was. I had a blank piece of paper and a completely incomprehensible brief, and so you get work, you get a phone conversation and, you know, you get, a rubber stamp, all you need to do is what's expected of you.

You write the brief in your own language.

We worked, in this kind of work, we can't look into the corporate side of things, the classic corporate communications type of thing . . . whereas in an agency it's like being a piece of meat chucked to the dogs sometimes and they're hungry dogs.

There's a sort of them and us, corporate agencies and innovation agencies . . . And that's partly because venture capital got in the way and tried to move everybody who's got a salary upstairs, so there's loads of energy, lots of good stuff coming out, but there's no continuity, there's no kind of thrust in new ideas and you know radical new ideas, and the whole industry was driven by that.

When the client wields so much power that you can't turn around and go, no, this is really good, it's going to work for you, and they go and the whole agency goes . . . you can't, you, know, the industry's f***ed.

Quite interesting from a client's side as well, what you said earlier about being paid for thinking, for ideas, I think that what clients pick by instinct are personalities, and a lot of the time clients are buying a relationship – you'll have a pitch to sell on personality.

I agree with that, the relationship has always been there. Obviously you do get major personalities, with major causes, for major relationships. It's always been there, but we're only starting to think about it.

It's interesting to have this conversation because I think in branding it's a tad different in that usually in terms of a piece of work you work on the brand and then maybe that brand will then go to a marketing, advertising agency, so I think that when you're developing or creating a brand there's more of an input for putting your personality or personality shape in there.

The group (not surprisingly) became very animated when asked to show their best pieces of work. The first pieces of work (three pieces in all) were from a creative in his late thirties, an experienced and confident man with a calm, laid-back personality.

The other thing I want to show you is we did a campaign for the National Railway Museum. I had to go up there and have a look round before we planned the campaign, and railway museum is somewhere I wouldn't normally go, but I was really kind of knocked over by the trains and all the stuff there, and I wanted to kind of convey some of that to people and so we did a whole campaign, and I actually got the sign writer who did the lettering on some of those carriages, and it actually did increase the number of people going to the museum. And the last piece is for an opera. I think this is good because it sort of sums up part of the beauty and a kind of ragged . . . I created it as a poster, and then had it printed as a poster, and stuck it up on concrete and then distressed it.

For this creative, the satisfaction in the pieces of work came from learning something new about the brand, and (in the second instance) from producing something which was in itself creative and evocative. Note the almost surprised tone in the statement that the advertising 'actually did increase the number of people going to the museum'.

The next piece of work was from a young team of creatives (in their early twenties) who had produced an online game to promote a sporting event. In the manner typical of a creative team, they told the story together, alternating the sentences.

> (Creative 1) We sort of pushed the boundaries slightly on the brief we'd been given, which was to find an online way to selling the Guardian Life Cup, we incorporated a drop-down banner. All the scores were updated on all the drop-down banners anywhere on the web, so you either went on the Team America or Team Europe, and so the scores which country or which subcontinent won, and . . . (Creative 2) I don't say it's our best piece of work but I say it's like, one that's quite personal, and also it's an idea that like, we got challenged by the client to do it, and they said, (Creative 1) Yeah, cool, do it. (Creative 2) It was good fun too because again it's not linear, it's not a piece of paper, it's not something . . . It's something you look at, and 10,000 people went there and played with it and interacted with it, (Creative 1) I mean that's brilliant, and you can see something.

In their case, the promotional material reflected their relative youth and their connection with other young people who would use the website. It is unlikely that anyone else in the room would have created anything like this (and it is entirely possible that most of them would not have known where to begin).

The next piece of work has become iconic for advertising creatives. The various campaigns for telecoms provider Orange have been widely acclaimed throughout the industry.

> The piece of work that I brought, the reason that it connects with me on a personal level, is Orange. It was a defining moment for what subsequently developed, and I really liked this idea that the whole essence of Orange at the time was about a brand, or a product – it was a personality, it was a child moving into the future, and that's what connects for me.

The study reported here demonstrates the extent to which the personalities of the creatives have a very clear influence on the work they produce (as might be expected). As creative people, they have a direct connection to the concept of diversity – they earn their living from being different, from thinking differently and from developing new ways of looking at things. The problem for advertising creatives is that they often want to input more of their personality than their clients will allow them to.

Conclusion

Individual personality and the diversity that this brings are obviously a positive and a negative factor in organisations. Personality differences can create conflicts, and in fact frequently do, which in many cases leads managers to resist allowing diversity. In fact, what this short-sighted approach fails to take account of is the fact that conflict is not necessarily a bad thing since conflict can lead to creative solutions.

Advertising creatives provide us with an extreme example. Creativity is what they are about: it is the lifeblood of their work as well as their individual personalities, so their systems of working are designed to exploit diversity (and hence conflict) in order to generate a dynamic, creative atmosphere. Creatives typically work in teams of two, and say openly that their best work comes about when they are teamed with someone who has a different approach to work and life. This illustrates the positive aspects of difference in which it becomes something which leads to growth, creative solutions and progress for the organisation.

Individual difference can, however, have a negative impact, notably in advertising creatives' relationships with advertising agencies and clients. Creatives who are too far out of step with the agency or the client simply find that their work is rejected, and they are forced off the job. This is the downside of personality difference – the area where being overtly different from the others will lead to a definite disadvantage. The natural upshot of this is, of course, that clients will tend to pick teams or agencies that fit in with their own views rather than seek out those who are different. In turn, this encourages agencies (and creatives) to become foxes (or chameleons) and fit in with what is expected rather than actually do something truly creative. For the creatives working on the account, this often means looking for ways to rewrite the brief in order to maintain their professional and personal integrity.

References

Bartlett, D. and Payne, S. (1997). Grounded Theory – Its Basis, Rationale and Procedures. In: *Understanding Social Research; Perspectives on Methodology and Practice*. Eds. McKenzie, G., Powell, J., and Usher, R., London: Falmer Press, pp. 173–195.

Corbin, J. and Strauss, A. (1990). Grounded Theory Research: Procedures, Canons and Evaluative Criteria. *Qualitative Sociology*, 13(1), pp. 3–21.

Daft, R. L. (1998). *Organisation Theory and Design*, Sixth Edition. Ohio: South Western College.

Hatch, M. J. (1997). *Organisation Theory – Modern Symbolic and Postmodern Perspectives*. Oxford: University Press.

Hellreigel, D. and Slocum, J. W. Jr. (1988). *Management*, Fifth Edition. London: Addison-Wesley.

Hochschild, A. R. (2003). *The Managed Heart: Commercialisation of Human Feeling*. Berkeley: University of California Press.

Hodge, B. J. and Anthony, W. P. (1991). *Organisation Theory – A Strategic Approach*, Fourth Edition. London: Allyn and Bacon.

Reitz, H. J. (1977). *Behavior in Organisations*. Homewood, IL: Richard D. Irwin.

Ruekert, Robert W. and Walker, Orville C. Jr. (1987). Marketing's Interaction with Other Functional Units: A Conceptual Framework and Empirical Evidence. *Journal of Marketing*, 51(January), pp. 1–19.

Chapter 5

Personality communicated in children's digital and non-digital drawings

Inferences for marketing research[*]

Judi Harris

Introduction

Albert Szent-Györgyi, the 1937 Nobel laureate whose research focused on the composition, isolation and nutritional uses of vitamin C, was known to have said, 'Discovery consists of seeing what everybody has seen and thinking what nobody has thought' (Buettner and Schafer, 2006, p. 6). This chapter will describe an illustration of Szent-Györgyi's maxim in applying the results of research about the communicative aspects of children's artwork to emerging inquiry about personality-sensitive design in marketing.

A commonly held understanding among educators and psychologists is that people communicate aspects of themselves and their experiences symbolically in their artistic works (Carini, 2007; Hunsley et al., 2015). Teachers, especially those working with children and pre-adolescents, are encouraged to use every source of information available to help them to understand their pupils' learning needs and preferences as completely as possible: observations of students' behaviour; the content of their writing; their parents' comments; the error patterns evident in their assignments; their test scores; and also the characteristics of their creative works. These holistic, continuing observations can be used to customise and personalise young students' learning.

Teachers can become frustrated with educational researchers' apparent lack of awareness of how well many know their students, how they build that knowledge and how they use it to assist students' learning. The longtime use of collaborative, systematic child study processes, such as Carini's (1979) highly structured 'descriptive review' of children's art, writing and mathematical problem-solving, demonstrates that teachers can and have gleaned important information about their own and other teachers' students by examining and reflecting systematically upon the students' works together. The educational research described in this chapter was designed, in a sense, with hopes of validating the reality of this 'practitioners' truth' – to discover what, if any, verifiable information viewing teachers can accurately infer about young artists by examining their graphic creations, but without knowledge of the children who produced them.

The study's results were shared with educational researchers through publication (Harris, 1997) and presentation. As Szent-Györgyi's statement describes, the 'discovery' here – that is the creative cross-disciplinary connection that Professor Moss made upon finding and reading my research – is the possibility that a study of what children's drawings communicate may point the way to similarly focused and productive research in marketing. If children's artwork reflects much personal information to teachers who have never met the young artists, then it is possible that marketing images (e.g. logos and other designs) also reflect aspects of their creators.

Given the importance of mirroring to determine consumer choices (Barry, 2009), and rooted in the empathy principle of aesthetic experience (Crozier and Greenhalgh, 1992), the potential link in marketing preferences between the personalities of the creator and the observer could be worthy of study. This chapter focuses on evidence for a link between artists' personal characteristics and graphic expression, while later chapters in the book (Chapters 6–9) focus on the roles of creators' and observers' personalities in shaping preferences.

Brands as communicative works

Brands – names and/or symbols intended to identify and differentiate goods or services from each other (Aaker, 1991) – are said to have 'personalities', in that they are associated with sets of human characteristics that serve symbolic or self-expressive functions for consumers. Brand personality characteristics, including demographics such as gender, age, ethnicity and class, can become associated with brands through brand symbols or logos (Batra, Lehmann and Singh, 1993; Aaker, 1997). The greater the congruity between a brand's personality and a consumer's notions of actual or ideal self, the greater the probability for purchase (Aaker, 1997; Karande, Zinkhan and Lum, 1997). Those consumer selves – once thought to be expressed consistently over time and across contexts – are actually rather 'malleable', influenced by schematic (e.g. sex or age) and situational self-perceptions (Aaker, 1999) and perceived changes in brand personalities. Brand characteristics are developed and communicated consciously by marketers, both directly and symbolically, as part of the overall marketing strategy for a product, but can be experienced differently by dissimilar consumers and over time (Johar, Sengupta and Aaker, 2005).

Might some aspects of a brand's personality be communicated through its symbols or logo *without* marketers' conscious intent? Design scholarship points to the probability of this phenomenon. Buchanan (1995), for example, in tracing the history of design by examining the rhetoric of products – 'the study of how products come to be as vehicles of argument and persuasion about the desirable qualities of private and public life' (p. 26) – concludes that 'products embody the intentions and purposes of their makers' (p. 55). Some empirical research results also demonstrate the reality of brands' embodied qualities vis-à-vis their designers. Moss's study of adult males' and females' designs and design preferences (1995), for example, showed strong and significant 'like for like' tendencies: both men and women preferred designs created by designers of the same sex as viewers. Later research by Moss (1999), Moss and Colman (2001), Moss, Gunn and Heller (2006) and Moss and Gunn (2009) replicated these findings with both designer and non-designer participant samples, using a variety of designed products, from business cards to holiday greetings to websites. Moss (1996, 2009) relates these results to examples of successful brands and their designers, suggesting that one way of increasing sales among women may be either to hire more female brand designers, who – unknowingly – communicate gender-specific design features, or to hire designers of either sex who demonstrate clear understanding of a female brand aesthetic.

This notion of subconscious communication of aspects of self is what is central to the possibility of personal projections in artists' and designers' works. Consumer research has explored the symbolic meanings of products, and found them to be often quite social in nature (Karande, Zinkhan and Lum, 1997). This means that goods and services can be seen as tools that are used to communicate indirectly with consumers. Specifically, a product's visual representations, described here as artistic works, can be seen to contain information that evokes an aesthetic response from the consumer. This response, which is a form of multilayered, simultaneous discourse due to the brand representations' symbolic nature, is based in a unique personified relationship between the spectator and the work. This 'empathy principle' of the psychology of aesthetic experience is 'a dynamic process that takes place between object and spectator . . . [who] identifies with the object [and] becomes, so to speak, fused with it' (Crozier and Greenhalgh, 1992, p. 74).

A similar principle is echoed in work about visual culture. Rogoff's (1998) examination of scholarship in this field, for example, depicts the visual as inextricably linked with verbal, auditory, emotional, physical, intellectual, spatial and historical attributes and responses. Thus, to understand images (and therefore marketing visuals) in postmodernity, their perception and reception must be explored in terms of the 'cultural, social, and economical conditions surrounding [their] producers and users' (Fischman, 2001, p. 29) – and as acts that are both passive and active for both designer and consumer.

The empathy principle, therefore, could well explain the primary mechanism by which artworks' viewers respond to what they see and otherwise sense. Certainly, the results of the study presented here suggest that children's artistic creations may communicate much more about their artists than generally assumed. If similar findings are found to be true on a larger scale, and with adults' graphic designs, they have broad implications for design as it relates to marketing to target populations.

Drawings as psychological communication

Moss and colleagues' work with adult male and female designers draws upon a considerable body of educational and psychological literature about children's drawings in the absence of sufficiently triangulated scholarship to date about projective aspects of marketing images. Most research about the interpretation of drawings as communicative devices examines either children's works or adults' creations. A notable exception, however, is Silver's work in art therapy (1987, 1992, 1993, 2001). In studies with large (300- to 700-members) and heterogeneous samples, using standardised 'stimulus drawing' tasks and well-validated scoring instruments with high inter-rater reliabilities, artists' expressions of emotion, self-image, attitudes towards self and others, and depictions of relationships were consistently and significantly differentiated by sex and age, as perceived by researchers when viewing participants' drawings and corresponding titles. Each of Silver's studies was completed with approximately equal numbers of participants from four different age groups: children, adolescents, younger adults and the elderly. This work suggests that artists of every age similarly express personal information via their works, and the content and nature of these unconscious communications differ significantly by age and sex. Is more information about artists, beyond sex and age, also expressed in their creations? Extant research has explored answers to this question more with children than adults to date.

The study and use of children's drawings as personally communicative devices have a long and rich history in educational inquiry. Drawing 'is broadly recognized as a visual language that helps children communicate with others', and is being explored by researchers increasingly as a highly situated, 'sociocultural semiotic *activity*' (Papandreou, 2014, p. 88, emphasis added). The tendency to regard the act of drawing as a meaning-making activity, rather than as a means to an end (the drawing), is becoming prevalent in research about children's drawings. This is because

> Language as a communicational medium is inadequate for the expression of everything that we think, feel or sense. Hence, drawing, graphic-narrative play and other forms of artistic expression offer important and distinct forms of meaning-making through figurative communication, which is intricate, multifaceted, symbolic and metaphoric.
>
> (Wright, 2007, p. 24)

Thus, exploration of the communicative functions of children's drawing has expanded to include examination both of what children intend to communicate (e.g. Hall, 2010) and what is embedded subconsciously in their artwork. These subconscious statements about children's selves and relationships are communicated via their drawings and have been researched primarily with reference to the artists' psychosocial characteristics that the drawings are thought to reveal.

There is a long history to the investigation of the content of children's drawings. They were first presented as potential psychologically diagnostic tools when Corrado Ricci, an art critic with interests in psychology, published the first known reproductions of children's art in 1887. A number of other scholarly studies of children's sketches followed (Klepsch and Logie, 1982), and these led to Goodenough's (1926) seminal work, which presented the first systematised method for estimating artists' intelligence from drawings of people. This technique was standardised and embellished by Harris (1963) and Harris and Roberts (1972), resulting in the Goodenough–Harris instrument. Dubbed the 'Draw-a-Man Test' since the task presented to the child is quite simply one of drawing a man, this is the earliest example of a class of open-ended drawing investigations called human figure drawings (HFDs), which have since been incorporated into several standardised intelligence and psychological tests for children. Most psychological research with children's drawings completed to date has made use of the HFD or one of its variants.

Among practising psychologists and educators, it is generally accepted that children's drawings have both 'projective' and 'non-projective' uses in psychological assessment. 'Projection' is a clinical term used in this context to suggest that an artist unconsciously imbues the picture being drawn with self-perceptions, regardless of the intended focus for the work. There are four types of projections thought to be observable in children's drawings: those that symbolically communicate aspects of personality; perceptions of self in relation to others; and the artists' values and specific attitudes. Non-projective indicators in children's artwork include those that 'measure a child's developmental or intellectual maturity' (Klepsch and Logie, 1982, p. 13).

Ninety years of research into projective and non-projective assessment of children's drawings suggest that it is possible for artist characteristics such as intellectual acuity, developmental maturity, personality, values, attitudes, emotions, behaviour and culture of origin to be discerned by systematic viewing of children's artistic works (LaVoy et al., 2001; Milne, Greenway and Best, 2005). Indeed, as Carini's decades of research with teachers' interpretations of children's creations demonstrates, 'what people make, child or adult, has meaning and importance – that the work bears the imprint of the maker – and that these meanings and the maker's hand are visible in the work' (2007, p. 4). Practitioners are cautioned, however, not to use such measures alone for psychological diagnosis, since children's works can be reflective of transient emotional states and attitudes towards the topics depicted visually (Thomas and Jolley, 1998), and the reliability and validity of specific picture elements' correlations with particular psychopathologies are not always consistent across artists (Lilienfeld, Wood and Garb, 2000) or clinicians (Jolley, 2010). Moreover, the validity of projective drawing techniques as psychological assessment tools has long been a controversial topic, given the lack of sufficient standardisation in administering, interpreting and scoring children's drawings, especially across the many variations of the HFD test (Hunsley, Lee, Wood and Taylor, 2015). In practice, projective drawings 'maintain their place in the armamentarium of many psychologists', despite some assertions as to 'the paucity of scientific evidence for their usefulness' (Hunsley, Lee, Wood and Taylor, 2015, p. 62), because clinicians report their utility in assisting with socioemotional diagnoses when used in combination with other formal and informal measures.

Professionals who analyse the projective and non-projective content of children's drawings are trained to assess the works according to the specific protocols of the particular HFD instrument that is being used for psychological assessment. In this study, however, a set of questions was created to explore the possibility of *untrained* viewers' accurate assessments of the symbolic content of children's drawings:

- Can teachers recognise and identify individual artists' traits correctly from viewing their artwork?
- Which artist traits are correctly and incorrectly identified?
- Does the accuracy of these informal assessments vary according to the different media that children used to create their pictures?

Viewers' training

A sizable body of literature has been directed towards establishing the validity of human figure drawing (HFD) instrument variants, some of which make use of untrained or 'naive' judges. Several studies include teachers in this category. In summarising the research on trained and untrained judges' interpretive abilities, Swensen (1968) concluded that 'formal training is not particularly related to success in interpreting the Draw-A-Person Test' (p. 39), even though some studies do show statistically significant differences between the assessments of trained psychologists and untrained teachers (e.g. Tolor, 1955). Hiler and Nesvig (1965) suggest that 'well-developed intuitive ability rather than formal clinical training is of primary importance in the interpretation of figure drawings' (p. 526).

The study described in this chapter explored that possibility. If human beings use intuitive processes to detect and respond to verifiable information about artists by looking at their works, perhaps teachers use information garnered intuitively when viewing children's creations as one of many ways to get to know their students. Given this function for intuitively received impressions, what characterises the process of teachers' intuitive knowing in educational contexts?

This question is easier asked than answered. In reviewing education's definitions of and responses to the notion of teachers' intuition, Claxton (2000) summarised it as a 'loose-knit family of "ways of knowing" which are less articulate and explicit than normal reasoning and discourse' (p. 49). These ways of knowing include:

- functioning 'fluently and flexibly in complex domains without being able to describe or theorize one's expertise';
- extracting 'intricate patterns of information that are embedded in a range of seemingly disparate experiences';

- making 'subtle and accurate judgements based on experience without . . . justification';
- detecting and extracting 'the significance of small, incidental details of a situation that others may overlook';
- taking time to 'mull over problems in order to arrive at more insightful or creative solutions';
- and applying 'this perceptive, ruminative, inquisitive attitude to one's own perceptions and reactions'.

(p. 50)

How do educators put such knowing into action? Noddings and Shore (1984) chose to characterise intuitive modes by involvement of both external and internal senses; by a relaxation of distancing into receptivity; by a quest for understanding or insight; and by a continuing tension between subjective certainty and objective uncertainty (p. 89).

The extent to which 'untrained' (or intuitive) observers are able to reach, maintain and deepen such states as they review children's drawings may predict how accurately they perceive verifiable information about the drawings' artists. This could suggest how the results of the study described ahead might inform future marketing research, development and practice.

Study type

How, then, might we test the accuracy of information received intuitively about child artists by observers of their works? The following two research questions were formed to organise this study:

- What is the scope of verifiable information communicated to teachers through children's digital and freehand drawings?
- How, if at all, do the scope and/or accuracy of information communicated through children's artwork differ when different drawing tools are used?

Results that address these questions, and ways in which the answers may relate to the communicative aspects of marketing images, are presented ahead. A more detailed description of the findings is available in Harris (1997).

A word on research questions follows, before describing the study's design in more detail. According to Yin (2014), all research questions can be classified as 'who', 'what', 'where', 'why' or 'how' queries. 'Who', 'what' and 'where' questions are often refined to 'how many' and 'how much' questions, which are best approached with quantitative measures, especially when predictive results are desired. 'What' questions can be approached with any research strategy. 'How' and 'why' questions, asked about contemporary situations over which the researcher has little or no control, are often best explored with case studies. Yin is careful to note that the most frequently cited drawback of case studies – that they are not generalisable to larger populations – reflects a misunderstanding of the intent of case study research. According to Yin, case study results, 'like experiments', are generalisable to theoretical propositions and not to populations or universes. In this sense, the case study, like the experiment, does not represent a 'sample', and the investigator's goal is to expand and generalise theories, which is analytic generalisation, rather than enumerating frequencies, which can be done as part of statistical generalisation (Yin, 2014, p. 21).

Stake (1995) recommends in-depth, case-based studies as the preferred method for social science inquiry because 'they may be epistemologically in harmony with the reader's experience and thus to that person a natural basis for generalisation' (p. 5), and are therefore more directly relevant to practitioners in fields such as education and social work. Yin (2014) similarly recommends the case study for empirical inquiry that investigates a contemporary phenomenon within its real-life context when the boundaries between the phenomenon and its context are not clearly evident. Research foci for such empirical exploration, like the focus explored in this study, often constitute new connections and directions in research-based inquiry.

Yin (2014) also suggests that multiple case study designs be conceptualised similarly to multiple, repeated experiments, following 'a replication, not a sampling logic' (p. 63). Accordingly, Yin recommends, multiple data types from multiple sources should be generated for each case, then interpreted and summarised as if each case were a separate study before any cross-case analysis is begun. These research design recommendations formed the basis from which the specific methods for data generation and analysis were selected to explore answers to the two research questions presented earlier.

Study design

To explore the verifiable information communicated in children's drawings, and how it might differ by artists, viewers and/or media, multi-source, open-ended techniques were used to generate data about the artists in the study. Teachers' impressions of young artists' personal characteristics were solicited in response to their viewing of the children's artistic works. These impressions were compared with the perceptions of the personal characteristics and preferences of the child artists as expressed by parents, the children's teachers and the artists themselves, obtained through semi-structured interviews. Coded interviews from all participants (children, parents and the children's teachers) and intuited impressions from teachers viewing the children's works, therefore, made up the data for each case in this study.

Two overarching types of data analysis were completed. The first was a comparison of two forms of data generated about the artists: the content of the interviews versus the viewing teachers' impressions of the children, garnered from their drawings. This first comparison revealed the proportion of information inferred by the teachers from the artists' drawings that could be confirmed by interview data. The other overarching type of data analysis explored variations in information communicated about the artists that could be discerned when different teachers' perceptions, varied drawing media and diverse artists' works were compared. Since this was an exploratory study, the logical/analytical conclusions sought were understood to be tentative in character, as recommended earlier by Yin.

The study used a purposive and convenience sample of child artists, comprising ten gifted fifth-grade boys who were US citizens with at least one parent who had a post-baccalaureate degree. Miles and Huberman (1994) recommend the use of a purposive sample in exploratory, in-depth studies such as this one 'because social processes have a logic and coherence that random sampling of events or treatments usually reduces to uninterpretable sawdust' (p. 36). Patton (2002) suggests that researchers select cases to study that promise the most cogent information about the topic of investigation. He recommends that these be 'critical cases . . . [those that] make a point quite dramatically or are, for some reason, particularly important' (p. 102). Patton acknowledges that although studying one or a few critical cases does not technically permit broad generalisations to all possible cases, logical generalisations can often be made from the weight of the evidence produced in studying several cases or even a single, critical case.

Ten children agreed to be participants in this study. All were 9- or 10-year-old males in fifth grade in public elementary schools in a south-eastern US state when they were interviewed. All had been identified for their school districts' gifted and talented programmes and had qualified for a local university's summer enrichment programme for gifted and talented students. This high degree of demographic similarity was sought so that perceived differences among students might be maximally specific to individual participants' personal attributes. Each student was asked to select one parent and one teacher to be interviewed about their perceptions of the student. All names were changed to pseudonyms to protect informants' rights to confidentiality.

Data generation and analysis

All study data were generated with the study's 44 participants: 10 children artists, 10 parents, 10 of the children's teachers and 14 viewing teachers who did not know the artists. The semi-structured interviews of the students, parents and current classroom teachers, each of which was approximately one hour in length, were audiotaped and transcribed verbatim. The contents of these transcripts were then analysed by theme using Strauss and Corbin's (1998) recommended methods for grounded theory research. The Ethnograph software (1988) was used to organise coded data and surface within- and across-participant results.

All participants were asked to describe the students' most and least favourite school subjects, problem-solving methods, social interaction patterns, personal 'life philosophies' and activity preferences. Study participants provided information in response to all prompts, with the exception of several children who were not able to describe their own metacognitive problem-solving processes. Lists of statements about the artists – each containing one discrete idea (the study's unit of analysis) – were created for each interview by the researcher, using participants' words whenever possible. Considered together, the lists contained all of the content relevant to the interview prompts in the study. Member checking was done by surface mail, asking individual study participants to read and correct any interpretive discrepancies made by the researcher in the lists of summarised statements about the students. Of the 1,397 statements that were written and sent to informants, all were read and returned. Fifty-one statements were corrected with respect to content (6 statements) and wording (47 statements). Overall, only a small fraction – approximately 4% – of the statements were corrected by study participants.

Constant comparative coding (Strauss and Corbin, 1998) revealed 15 mutually exclusive theme categories across interview statement lists. Coding reliability and validity were ensured by frequent meetings with two peer debriefers and the maintenance and review of the researcher's reflexive methodological log (Lincoln and Guba, 1985). One peer debriefer also reviewed all information generated for a randomly selected case, comparing it to the researcher's data analysis for the same case, to ensure that summary statements were firmly grounded in generated data.

Immediately prior to being interviewed, each student informant drew three pictures – one in each of three different media. The content and style of the pictures were determined completely by the students; the only instructions given by the researcher regarded the media to use for each drawing. Participants had a choice of crayons, magic markers and coloured pencils to use for the freehand picture; a touch-sensitive graphics tablet (Touch Window, 1985) and digital drawing software (Animation Station, 1984) for the picture made with the tablet; and their choice of either IBM Logo (1983), Apple Logo II (1984) or LogoWriter (1986) software for the Logo picture. All computer-assisted pictures were drawn on Apple IIe computers, with the exception of one Logo picture created on an IBM PC. All of the students had learned to use Logo before participating in this study.

Participants gave the researcher permission to keep the pictures the students created and show them to teachers who had not met the children. Two groups of teachers viewed the pictures and responded to them. One group, comprising five teachers, was graduate students taking a summer Logo course in New York, and the others (nine teachers) were graduate students completing Logo-based coursework during the same summer session in Oregon. All had previously worked with Logo with elementary-aged children in instructional settings. The two graduate course instructors received 35-mm slide reproductions of the children's pictures, arranged in a standard order in a slide carousel, and sufficient copies of a paper-based viewer response form to provide one for each of the graduate students in their classes. The instructors were then asked to follow the viewing instructions printed on the first page of the response form. Pictures formed with similar media were grouped together in a slide carousel, but the artist order in each media-related group was different. Viewers were told only that children drew the 30 pictures; they did not know that ten artists produced all of the works, nor did they know anything about each child's age, gender, computer experience or exceptionality.

Two types of information were requested of the viewing teachers: demographic data (age and sex) and impressions of the students' behaviour patterns, learning styles, school subject preferences and any other information that occurred to the viewing teachers. All viewing teachers but one completed the response forms in full. Given the prevalence of research about children's drawings that reports on perceived age and sex, the results shared here will address the accuracy of the viewing teachers' impressions of other perceived artist characteristics.

The contents of all viewing teachers' response forms were rewritten as lists of statements about the student artists, following the same procedure used to process interview data, as described earlier. These lists of statements were then analysed using constant comparative techniques for data analysis (Strauss and Corbin, 1998), yielding eight mutually exclusive coding categories. Answers to both specific and open-ended questions – in the form of lists of statements about each of the ten artists – on the viewer response form were compared with interview data to determine agreement or lack thereof.

Levels of agreement between viewing teachers' comments and interview data were classified as 'agree', 'disagree', 'agree by implication', 'disagree by implication' or 'not mentioned'. If the content of a particular viewer's statement about an artist was mentioned in two or more interviews with people who knew the artist (parent, teacher, self), the statement was assumed to agree with interview data. If the obverse of the content of a particular viewer conjecture was mentioned in two or more interviews, the viewing teacher's statement was assumed to disagree with interview data. If the content was implied but not stated directly in interview data from at least two people who knew the artist, it was assumed to agree by implication. Similarly, if the content of a viewer comment was countered indirectly in two or more interviews, then it was assumed to disagree by implication. If the content of a particular viewer comment or its opposite was mentioned in only one interview about the artist, it was not tallied. Finally, if the content of a viewer conjecture about an artist was not mentioned directly or indirectly in any interview with study participants who knew the artist, it was listed as 'not mentioned'.

This process was checked for accuracy by one of the study's peer debriefers, who selected a case at random, and traced the claims made in the results summary back to the data generated for the study. This admittedly strict strategy for assessing levels of agreement between viewing teachers' statements and interview data was used to ensure the robustness of the study's results.

Results

The study's results are described ahead, summarised first across participants, and then separated by drawing media and individual artists and teachers. Variations among viewing teachers' perceptions are also presented. The viewing teachers' years of experience teaching, using computers as personal/professional tools, teaching children with computers, programming in Logo and helping their students to program in Logo are presented first in Table 5.1 to help to contextualise the study results that follow. As Table 5.1 shows, the teachers who viewed children's artwork in this study had a broad and varied range of educational and technology experience.

Viewers' perceptions of the artists

A total of 595 viewer-supplied comments were written about the artists of the 30 pictures. Viewing teachers were given virtually unlimited space in which to write their open-ended perceptions. There was little difference in the percentages of open-ended comments supplied for the works of different individual artists. Jon's work received 8% of viewer comments on the lower end of the continuum, and Drew's pictures received 13% of the viewers' voluntary comments on the opposite end. However, although the numbers of comments supplied for different artists did not vary that much, percentages of viewer-supplied comments that could be substantiated with interview data were quite different for different artists (see Table 5.2).

Table 5.1 Viewing teachers' professional experience.

Years spent	Teachers													
	A	B	C	D	E	F	G	H	I	J	K	L	M	N
Teaching	15	5	6	11	4	5	17	18	27	25	15	32	5	8
Computers	10	4	3	5	3	8	15	8	10	6	10	14	2	5
Children	8	4	2	2	3	4	10	8	10	4	8	9	2	2
Logo	6	1	1	1	3	3	8	5	6	4	4	2	2	1
w/Children	4	1	1	1	3	3	8	5	5	2	4	1	2	1
Total	43	15	13	20	16	23	58	44	58	41	41	58	12	17

Note: Total years teaching ('Teaching'); years using computers ('Computers'); years using computers when teaching children ('Children'); years programming in Logo ('Logo'); years using Logo with children ('w/Children'). 'Total' represents column tallies provided only for comparison among participating teachers; they have no true mathematical value.

Table 5.2 Numbers of comments (n) supplied about artists, classified by accordance with interview data.

Artist	n	Relationship to interview data		
		Agreement	Disagreement	Not mentioned
Drew	78	54 (69%)	13 (17%)	11 (14%)
Mark	60	43 (72%)	12 (20%)	5 (8%)
Lance	59	40 (68%)	12 (20%)	7 (12%)
Jon	49	31 (63%)	10 (21%)	8 (16%)
James	55	41 (75%)	10 (18%)	4 (7%)
Sid	62	47 (76%)	10 (16%)	5 (8%)
Bruce	56	33 (59%)	16 (28%)	7 (13%)
Rick	56	33 (68%)	13 (23%)	5 (9%)
Herb	67	46 (69%)	16 (24%)	5 (7%)
Harvey	53	36 (68%)	16 (30%)	1 (2%)

Table 5.3 Number of comments (n) written by viewing teachers, classified by accordance with interview data.

Teachers	n	Relationship to interview data		
		Agreement	Disagreement	Not mentioned
A	112	35 (76%)	24 (21%)	3 (3%)
B	25	15 (60%)	6 (24%)	4 (16%)
C	23	12 (52%)	6 (26%)	5 (22%)
D	7	5 (71%)	2 (29%)	0 (0%)
E	11	7 (64%)	1 (9%)	3 (27%)
F	15	13 (87%)	2 (13%)	0 (0%)
G	124	93 (75%)	22 (18%)	9 (7%)
H	87	62 (71%)	20 (23%)	5 (6%)
I	67	41 (61%)	20 (30%)	6 (9%)
J	18	11 (61%)	5 (28%)	2 (11%)
K	Did not provide viewing data			
L	43	34 (71%)	12 (25%)	2 (4%)
M	22	13 (59%)	0 (0%)	9 (41%)
N	24	13 (54%)	2 (8%)	9 (38%)

The range of comments that agreed with interview data was 50%–76%; 16%–30% for comments that disagreed with interview data; and 2%–16% of the comments that were offered by viewers that did not appear in interview data.

Individual teachers' percentages of interview-substantiated open-ended comments ranged from 52% (Teacher C) to 87% (Teacher F), as shown in Table 5.3. These perceptual performance numbers were not paralleled by either years of teaching experience or correct perceptions of age and gender. Teacher E is the only teacher to perceive age, gender and viewer-supplied artist attributes similarly; her scores were close to the group's averages in each instance.

Moreover, although there were individual differences among viewing teachers concerning the total number of comments offered in response to the artwork, the teachers with the highest percentages of interview-substantiated comments were not those who also made the most conjectures.

Perceptions according to drawing media

Of the 595 total unprompted comments about the artists that were offered by the viewing teachers, 235 (39%) were inspired by viewing freehand drawings, 207 (35%) were offered in response to viewing pictures created with a touch-sensitive graphics tablet and 153 (26%) were recorded when looking at pictures created with Logo. Although freehand media seemed to catalyse more unprompted comments than graphics-tablet creations, and these pictures, in turn, inspired more viewer comments than Logo pictures, percentages of interview-substantiated artist perceptions were roughly equivalent (freehand: 68%; graphics tablet: 70%; Logo: 69%; see Table 5.4). This is particularly interesting considering that many viewers commented informally to their instructors that they felt as if they 'knew' the artists better when looking at their freehand drawings.

Overall, 69% of viewers' comments about the artists agreed with interview data, 21% disagreed with interview data and 10% were comments that were not mentioned in interviews by any of the three participants (artist, parent or teacher) giving information about a particular artist.

This research was a study of individuals: ten individual artists and the perceptions of 13 individual teachers. It explored whether certain aspects of the ten fifth graders' individualities were communicated to Logo-using teachers through free-form artistic works created in three different media. Although no statistical generalisations can be made from a multi-case, exploratory study with a comparatively small sample such as this one, patterns across participant groups and among individuals can be noted. These should be considered trustworthy for this particular group of study participants because of the methodological rigour demonstrated in data generation and analysis (Corbin and Strauss, 2015), as described earlier.

Results for individual students

Certainly no teacher or group of teachers in this study described any of the artists with the rich detail revealed by combining the students' self-reports with parental and classroom teacher interview data. On the other hand, the freehand and computer-facilitated artwork of seven of the ten child participants (Drew, Mark, Lance, Sid, James, Herb and Harvey; see Table 5.5) generated unique viewer comments and patterns of perceptions about the artists.

Table 5.4 Total numbers of verified statements (*n*) by viewing teachers, classified by drawing media and accordance with interview data.

Media used by artist	n	Relationship to interview data		
		Agreed	Disagreed	Not mentioned
Handheld drawing tools	235	159 (68%)	47 (20%)	29 (12%)
Graphics tablet	207	145 (70%)	42 (20%)	20 (10%)
Logo	153	106 (69%)	39 (25%)	8 (05%)

Table 5.5 Participating children's drawings, identified by pseudonym and classified by media type used.

Artist	Freehand drawing	Tablet drawing	Logo drawing
Bruce			
Drew			
Harvey			
Herb			
James			
Jon			
Lance			

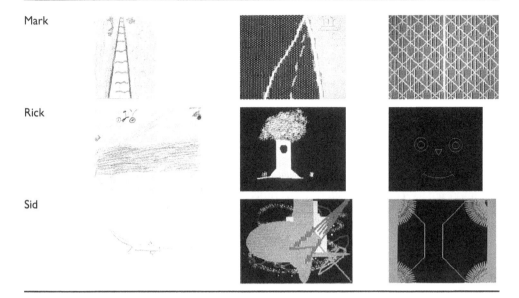

For example Drew was described as 'impatient with mistakes' and 'happy and serious'. Mark, it was suspected, 'combines and builds on knowledge', and was described as 'talkative' and 'security-oriented'. Lance's language arts proficiency, emphasising fine arts applications, was intuited by several viewing teachers; he was also one of only two children in this group who was described as 'generally a compliant kid'. James had 19 comments made in response to his drawings that mentioned neatness, concern with detail, precision and related work-habit attributes. Sid was portrayed by the viewing teachers as 'bold', 'adventuresome', 'restless', 'creative' and a 'divergent thinker'. Herb was suspected to have a 'strong personality', and to be a 'quiet', 'intense individual with definite goals'. Harvey's interests in science and animal study were mentioned by several viewers; he was also described as 'impulsive', 'in a hurry' and 'want[ing] to get it right'. These artists' works are displayed in Table 5.5, along with three other artists' sets of drawings.

Although these attributes do not fully portray each individual artist's uniqueness, they are characteristics that begin to differentiate the artists from each other as unique individuals. For example 'getting it right' was a characteristic mentioned about several of the children during interviews with parents and teachers (e.g. Drew and James), yet Harvey was the only artist whose artwork communicated attention to 'appearing right'. This paralleled the frequency with which this concern was voiced by his father and teacher.

More importantly, these distinguishing characteristics were indeed communicated through drawings to viewing teachers who had no other personal information available about the artists, along with other attributes (e.g. mathematics or science interest) that were more commonly perceived. Also, there were observable individual differences between children, such as Sid and James, who had the highest percentages of interview-substantiated viewer comments and Bruce, who had the lowest percentage of such comments. It is apparent that some of the children in this study were more or less 'readable' through their artwork than others were. It is difficult to suggest why that may be so.

It is interesting to note that eight of the ten student artists listed science as one of their preferred subjects in school, and seven of the ten mentioned mathematics as a favourite subject. These preferences were noted by many of the viewing teachers when they were considering pictures that the boys created in *all three media*. It would seem, therefore, that mathematics or science interest was not intuited primarily as a function of proficient use of a mathematically oriented medium, such as the Logo programming language. Rather, the content and/or forms of the images seemed to have prompted the viewing teachers' perceptions, regardless of digital or non-digital medium used.

It is also interesting to note that most viewer comments related to student work habits, such as being impatient with mistakes (Drew), wanting to 'get it right' (Harvey), neatness (James) and building on prior knowledge (Mark). The smallest proportion of viewing teachers' comments referred to students' physical features or capabilities. Also, any comments that were offered about emotional attributes or interpersonal behaviour patterns were 'positively' stated, or worded as apparent evidence of well-adjusted psychological orientations, even when several of the students had some emotional and interpersonal concerns voiced about them by the adults interviewed (e.g. Harvey, Herb and Lance). These three patterns of teachers' perceptions reflect a probable professional focus for the viewing teachers upon children's academic performance and work habits, as well as upon children's social and emotional characteristics that may influence their schoolwork. The viewing teachers' comments seemed to focus less upon the psychosocial aspects of the children's personalities. Based upon extant research about clinical uses of children's drawings summarised earlier, psychosocial information may be perceived in the children's drawings more readily by professionals other than teachers, such as psychologists.

As the results of this study indicate, much about the children who drew the images examined by the viewing teachers was perceived correctly – and therefore, arguably, was communicated successfully. As explained earlier, the communicative functions of children's drawings are well accepted by educators and psychologists, even while appropriate uses for the differing types of analyses of children's works (e.g. clinical diagnoses) are debated.

Discussion

Given the long history of using children's drawings for diagnostic purposes – something presumably underpinned by an assumed communicative function of the children's works – comparatively little research has examined the broader range of specifically what (and how) children's drawings communicate. A notable exception is Hall's (2010) doctoral thesis. In her analysis of the contents and purposes of nearly 800 drawings created by 14 kindergarten and grade 1 children in south-west England during an academic year, Hall found, by talking with the children as they drew, that they used the activity of drawing to construct and express their *identities* primarily, and secondarily, their sense of *power*. Their purposes in creating their drawings were both cognitive and affective, and were wide-ranging, determined in part by the changing contexts in which they drew the images (e.g. home or school) and the events that occurred in those contexts over time. Hall concluded that although drawing by children has four functions – perception, communication, invention and action – communication is 'the overarching function', because drawing functions as a visual language (p. 366). If what Hall discovered about children communicating their identities via their drawings is true for the broader population of child artists, perhaps we should not be surprised that the teachers in this study were able to discern considerable amounts of specific information about children's identities by examining their drawings.

Readers may wonder how probable it is that the patterns documented in this study of teachers' perceptions of children's artwork would also be observed in designs and designed objects. Part of the answer to this question rests with the probable communicative equivalence of children's and adults' artwork, which has been suggested by the use of both in the psycho-assessment literature reviewed earlier (e.g. Silver, 1987, 1992, 1993), with similar results across age groups.

Another part of the answer refers to the communicative equivalence of design and fine art creations. Scholars have linked design aesthetics to artistic production and perception for more than 80 years, beginning with Read's first publication of *Art and Industry* in 1934. Read was among the earliest of the twentieth-century design scholars to discuss the aesthetic in the functional directly, saying, 'objects designed primarily for use appeal to the aesthetic sensibility as abstract art', and the designer as artist, whose 'problem is to adapt the laws of symmetry and proportion to the functional form of the object that is being made' (Read, 1934, p. 49). Frascara (1988) summarises this notion by reminding us that graphic design and art have more in common with each other than simply promoting a visual aesthetic. Both design and art affect the behaviour, attitude and conduct of their respective audiences. Communication is the common denominator, and such semiotic exchange via visual media seems clearly worth the attention of marketing researchers and practitioners.

How, then, can we bridge these research results in education with knowledge that may assist scholarship in marketing? The unexpectedly high percentage (69%) of verifiable unprompted comments made by remotely located viewing teachers about ten student artists working with both digital and non-digital media in this study, considered in combination with the results of both educational and marketing research referenced in this and other chapters in this book, suggests a strong possibility that both digital and non-digital creations encode and communicate aspects of their creators.

Potentially important questions follow for design and marketing. Are *all* graphic creations linked to and/or reflective of aspects of their creators' personalities? If not, what causes differences in the extent to which they are linked? Which aspects of personality are communicated more clearly, and via which types of designs? Can such semiotic information about works' creators be intentionally shaped, masked or changed? The answers to questions such as these could direct productive, and eventually helpful, marketing research concerning the impact of personality on design.

This suggests two possible courses of action for marketing scholarship and practice as it relates to personality-sensitive design. Marketing researchers could first examine the extent to which design and media creations are imbued with attributes of their creators, and then examine the extent to which consumers' preferences for designs and media are enhanced when the personalities of creators and observers match. If these studies find evidence of strong links, then design and marketing organisations could identify target consumers' personality types, and seek out brand developers with attributes and/or sensibilities similar to those of the brand's target audiences.

Such action could open design and brand development work to the ever-growing diversity of consumer populations. In following these suggestions, marketing professionals would be making and acting upon the kinds of discoveries that Szent-Györgyi (Buettner and Schafer,

2006) identified long ago, and with which this chapter began: those that result from seeing what everyone else sees, but thinking differently about it.

Note

* Note: An earlier version of this chapter was published in the *Journal of Brand Management*, volume 14, number 3 (Harris, 2007). Texts from that article are reproduced here with the permission of the journal's publisher, Palgrave Macmillan.

References

Aaker, DA 1991, *Managing brand equity: Capitalizing on the value of brand name*. Free Press, New York.

Aaker, JL 1997, 'Dimensions of brand personality', *Journal of Marketing Research*, vol. 34, no. 3, pp. 347–356.

Aaker, JL 1999, 'The malleable self: The role of self-expression in persuasion', *Journal of Marketing Research*, vol. 36, no. 1, pp. 45–57.

Animation Station 1984, software, SunCom, Wheeling.

Apple II Logo 1984, software, Logo Computer Systems, New York.

Barry, AM 2009, 'Mirror neurons: How we become what we see', *Visual Communication Quarterly*, vol. 16, no. 2, pp. 79–89.

Batra, R, Lehmann, DL and Singh, D 1993, 'The brand personality component of brand goodwill: Some antecedents and consequences', in DA Aaker & A Biel (eds.), *Brand equity and advertising*. Lawrence Erlbaum, Hillsdale, NJ, pp. 83–96.

Buchanan, R 1995, 'Rhetoric, humanism, and design', in R Buchanan & V Margolin (eds.), *Discovering design – explorations in design studies*. University of Chicago Press, Chicago, pp. 23–66.

Buettner, GR & Schafer, FQ 2006, 'Albert Szent-Gyorgyi: Vitamin C identification', *The Biochemist*, vol. 28, no. 5, pp. 31–33.

Carini, PF 1979, *The art of seeing and the visibility of the person*. University of North Dakota Press, Grand Forks.

Carini, PF 2007, 'Made by hand', essay from speech, *The Prospect Review*, vol. 29(e), viewed 1 June 2016, http://www.sustainlv.org/wp-content/uploads/Made-by-Hand-Carini.pdf.

Claxton, G 2000, 'The anatomy of intuition', in T Atkinson & G Claxton (eds.), *The intuitive practitioner: On the value of not always knowing what one is doing*. Open University Press, Berkshire, pp. 32–52.

Corbin, J & Strauss, A 2015, *Basics of qualitative research: Techniques and procedures for developing grounded theory*, 4th edn. SAGE, Thousand Oaks.

Crozier, WR & Greenhalgh, P 1992, 'The empathy principle: Towards a model for the psychology of art', *Journal for the Theory of Social Behaviour*, vol. 22, no. 1, pp. 63–79.

The Ethnograph 1988, software, Qualis Research, Colorado Springs.

Fischman, GE 2001, 'Reflections about images, visual culture, and educational research', *Educational Researcher*, vol. 30, no. 8, pp. 28–33.

Frascara, J 1988, 'Graphic design: Fine art or social science?', *Design Issues*, vol. 5, no. 1, pp. 18–29.

Goodenough, F 1926, *Measurement of intelligence by drawings*. Harcourt, Brace & World, Chicago.

Hall, E 2010, The communicative potential of young children's drawings, doctoral thesis, University of Exeter, Exeter, viewed 1 June 2016, https://ore.exeter.ac.uk/repository/handle/10036/105041.

Harris, DB 1963, *Children's drawings as measures of intellectual maturity*. Harcourt, Brace and World, New York.

Harris, DB & Roberts, J 1972, *Intellectual maturity of children: Demographic and sociometric factors*, report no. 116, Vital and Health Statistics Series 11, U.S. Department of Health, Education, and Welfare, Washington, DC.

Harris, JB 1997, 'What do freehand and computer-facilitated drawings tell teachers about the children who drew them?', *Journal of Research on Computing in Education*, vol. 29, no. 4, pp. 351–369.

Harris, JB 2007, 'Personal projections in artists' works: Implications for branding', *Journal of Brand Management*, vol. 14, no. 3, pp. 295–312.

Hiler, E & Nesvig, D 1965, 'An evaluation of criteria used by clinicians to infer pathology from figure drawings', *Journal of Consulting Psychology*, vol. 29, no. 6, pp. 520–529.

Hunsley, J, Lee, CM, Wood, JM & Taylor, W 2015, 'Controversial and questionable assessment techniques', in SO Lilienfeld, SJ Lynn & JM Lohr (eds.), *Science and pseudoscience in clinical psychology*, 2nd edn. Guilford Press, London, pp. 42–82.

IBM Logo 1983, software, Logo Computer Systems, New York.

Johar, GV, Sengupta, J & Aaker, J 2005, 'Two roads to updating brand personality impressions', *Journal of Marketing Research*, vol. 42, no. 4, pp. 458–469.

Jolley, RP 2010, *Children and pictures: Drawing and understanding*. Wiley Blackwell, West Sussex.

Karande, K, Zinkhan, GM & Lum, AB 1997, 'Brand personality and self-concept: A replication and extension', *American Marketing Association Educators' Proceedings*, vol. 8, pp. 165–171.

Klepsch, M & Logie, L 1982, *Children draw and tell: An introduction to the projective uses of children's human figure drawings*. Brunner/Mazel, New York.

LaVoy, SK, Pedersen, WC, Reitz, JM, Brauch, AA, Luxenberg, TM & Nofsinger, CC 2001, 'Children's drawings: A cross-cultural analysis from Japan and the United States', *School Psychology International*, vol. 22, no. 1, pp. 53–63.

Lilienfeld, SO, Wood, JM & Garb, HN 2000, 'The scientific status of projective techniques', *Psychology Science in the Public Interest*, vol. 1, no. 2, pp. 27–66.

Lincoln, YS & Guba, EG 1985, *Naturalistic inquiry*. SAGE, Newbury Park.

LogoWriter for the Apple II 1986, software, Logo Computer Systems, New York.

Miles, MB & Huberman, AM 1994, *Qualitative data analysis: An expanded sourcebook*. SAGE, Thousand Oaks.

Milne, LC, Greenway, P & Best, F 2005, 'Children's behaviour and their graphic representation of parents and self', *Arts in Psychotherapy*, vol. 32, no. 2, pp. 107–119. Moss, G 1995, 'Differences in the design aesthetic of men and women: Implications for product branding', *Journal of Brand Management*, vol. 3, no. 3, pp. 51–61.

Moss, G 1996, 'Sex – the misunderstood variable', *Journal of Brand Management*, vol. 3, no. 5, pp. 296–305.

Moss, G 1999, 'Gender and consumer behaviour: Further explorations', *Journal of Brand Management*, vol. 7, no. 2, pp. 88–100.

Moss, G 2009, *Gender, design and marketing: How gender drives our perception of design and marketing*. Gower, Surrey.

Moss, G & Colman, AM 2001, 'Choices and preferences: Experiments on gender differences', *Journal of Brand Management*, vol. 9, no. 2, pp. 89–98. Moss, G & Gunn, RW 2009, 'Gender differences in website production and preference aesthetics: Preliminary implications for ICT in education and beyond', *Behaviour and Information Technology*, vol. 28, no. 5, pp. 447–460.

Moss, G, Gunn, RW & Heller, J 2006, 'Some men like it black, some women like it pink: Consumer implications of differences in male and female website design', *Journal of Consumer Behavior*, vol. 5, no. 4, pp. 328–341.

Noddings, N & Shore, PJ 1984, *Awakening the inner eye: Intuition in education*. Teachers College Press, New York.

Papandreou, M 2014, 'Communicating and thinking through drawing activity in early childhood', *Journal of Research in Childhood Education*, vol. 28, no. 1, pp. 85–100.

Patton, MQ 2002, *Qualitative research & evaluation methods*, 3rd edn. SAGE, Thousand Oaks.

Read, H 1934, *Art and Industry*. Sage Faber and Faber, London.

Rogoff, I 1998, 'Studying visual culture', in N Mirzoeff (ed.), *The visual culture reader*. Routledge, New York, pp. 3–26.

Silver, RA 1987, 'Sex differences in the emotional content of drawings', *Art Therapy*, vol. 4, no. 2, pp. 67–77.

Silver, RA 1992, 'Gender differences in drawings: A study of self-images, autonomous subjects, and relationships', *Art Therapy*, vol. 9, no. 2, pp. 85–92.

Silver, RA 1993, 'Age and gender differences expressed through drawings: A study of attitudes toward self and others', *Art Therapy*, vol. 10, no. 3, pp. 159–168.

Silver, RA 2001, *Art as language: Access to thoughts and feelings through stimulus drawings*. Brunner-Routledge Psychology Press, Philadelphia.

Stake, RE 1995, *The art of case study research*. SAGE, Thousand Oaks.

Strauss, A & Corbin, J 1998, *Basics of qualitative research: Techniques and procedures for developing grounded theory*, 2nd edn. SAGE, Thousand Oaks.

Swensen, C 1968, 'Empirical evaluations of human figure drawings: 1957–1966', *Psychology Bulletin*, vol. 70, no. 1, pp. 20–44.

Thomas, GV & Jolley, RP 1998, 'Drawing conclusions: A re-examination of empirical and conceptual bases for psychological evaluation of children from their drawings', *British Journal of Clinical Psychology*, vol. 37, no. 2, pp. 127–139.

Tolor, A 1955, 'Teachers' judgments of the popularity of children from their human figure drawings', *Journal of Clinical Psychology*, vol. 11, no. 2, pp. 158–162.

Touch Window 1985, computer peripheral, Touch Screens, Inc., Lilburn.

Wright, S 2007, 'Graphic-narrative play: Young children's authoring through drawing and telling', *International Journal of Education & the Arts*, vol. 8, no. 8, pp. 1–27.

Yin, RK 2014, *Case study research: Design and methods*, 5th edn. SAGE, Thousand Oaks.

Part 2

Preferences for design and marketing and the role of personality

Chapter 6

Personality and design and marketing preferences

Gloria Moss

Importance of design and advertising

Advertising and design have a central place in today's world. In July 2014, e-Marketer predicted that worldwide media advertising spending in 2014 would total $545.40 billion, an increase of 5.7% on the previous year (e-Marketer, 2014). This is a staggering sum (Hirsh et al., 2012), with some businesses spending up to 30% of their annual revenue on advertising. The significance of design is likewise recognised since it is thought to shape consumer reactions and behaviour (Hammer, 1995), providing a key source of differentiation (Schmitt and Simonson, 1997). In fact, its power is such that it is thought to shape perceptions of a product's usability (Hassenzahl, 2007), usefulness and ease of use (Van Iwaarden et al., 2004), shaping the time attended to something (Maughan et al., 2007) and shaping people's willingness to pay a price premium of up to 66% (Bloch et al., 2003; Van der Heijden, 2003; Hassenzahl, 2007). Indeed, with the product design field encompassing the functionality, ergonomics and aesthetics of a physical product (Coates, 2003), it is described as replacing nature 'as the dominant presence in human experience' (Buchanan, 1995, p. xii).

Aesthetic aspects shape a product's appearance, and these aspects can include materials, proportion, colour, ornamentation, shape, size and reflectivity (Lawson, 1983). In today's competitive marketplace, companies need to reflect on interactions with design and consumers' aesthetic preferences (Creusen et al., 2010, pp. 1437–1438). This interaction leads Buchanan (2001, p. 11) to speak of 'interaction design', an approach that seeks to understand the 'experience of human beings that make and use [products]', assisting a new understanding through 'an investigation of what makes a product useful, usable, and desirable'. In understanding consumer preferences, it is important to ascertain the role personality plays in preferences. In this chapter, we will provide a brief overview of the psychology of preference, reviewing the earlier literature on design and marketing preferences and then moving on to the role of personality in design and advertising preferences.

Interaction design

The concept of 'interaction design' fits within an 'interactionist' philosophy (Mischel, 1997) that accepts that individuals may view physical and social settings differently and may produce different 'life-spaces' and consumption behaviours (Gehrt and Yan, 2004). Since purchases offer a vehicle for self-expression (Karande et al., 1997), the philosophy allows for the fact that designers need to shape products around the 'unique and particular needs' of the customer (Hammer, 1995), with a heterogeneous designer population facilitating the delivery of desirable designs (Dell'Era et al., 2010). Unfortunately, an understanding of elements determining 'desirability' remains one of the 'weakest topics of design research today' (Buchanan, 2001, p. 16), reinforcing an earlier view that there has been relatively little investigation of how this variable [aesthetics] affects preferences for products (Veryzer, 1993); that a deeper knowledge of the area is lacking (Noble and Kumar, 2010), with no detailed, 'differentiated picture . . . sensitive to differences aligned with educational background and training and . . . aware of issues of gender and race' (Nixon, 1997).

While there are relatively few investigations of 'interaction design', details are widely available on the contrasting 'universalist' or Kantian approach. For example design guidelines presumed to apply universally and across all demographic groups include Maeda's *Laws of Simplicity* (2006) and Nielsen's design guidelines for homepage usability (2001). Research, moreover, underpinned by universalist assumptions includes studies identifying the non-conscious design processes, the so-called internal processing algorithms (IPAs), that produce positive reactions to design (Veryzer, 1993) as well as work to isolate the universal rules governing the impact of complexity and functionality on aesthetic preferences (Creusen et al., 2010). Regrettably, neither study segmented its findings by demographic variables despite the view that research should examine the role of biology and culture in the formation of IPAs (Veryzer, 1993). In fact, a similar deficit applies to studies of web design aesthetics since many are likewise rooted in a universalist paradigm (Veryzer, 1993; Schmitt and Simonson, 1997; Creusen et al., 2010).

In pursuit of greater balance, this chapter reviews the earlier literature on the role of personality in design and marketing preferences seeking to establish the priority that should be accorded to it. In fact, there exists a long tradition of research exploring the relationship between consumer personality and responses to advertising (LaBarbara et al., 1998) and, to a lesser extent, design (Read, 1958; Norman, 2004), with Norman stating that 'no single product can hope to satisfy everyone. The designer must know the audience for whom the product is intended' (Norman, 2004, p. 39). He goes on to say that 'Personality theorists divide people along such dimensions as extraversion, agreeableness, conscientiousness, emotional stability and openness. To designers, this means that "no single design will satisfy everyone"' (Norman, 2004, p. 39).

Norman speaks in fact of the necessity to achieve congruence between the 'designer's model' and the 'user's model' (p. 75), the mental model that the consumer has of the object, but no mention is made unfortunately of the part played by personality. The purpose of this chapter is to fill the gap through an overview of the literature on preferences, much of which comes from the early decades of the last century when these research questions were actively discussed. We will begin with some background on preferences.

The direction of preferences

What direction do people's preferences normally take? Do opposites attract, or do preferences generally follow a mirroring principle with like attracting like?

It might be useful if we look first at the case of social bonds and see the direction of preferences in this case. What we learn from the evidence is that both similarity and difference can be powerful engines for *rapprochement* and it is intriguing to establish which is the more dominant. The first view was expounded by George Kelly, originator of personal construct theory (vide Chapter 1) in his two-volume work *The Psychology of Personal*

Constructs (1955, p. 7). There he writes, 'Man looks at his world through transparent templates which he creates and then attempts to fit over the realities of which the world is composed.' He went on to suggest that people develop relationships with people to the extent that the other person has a similar way of looking at the world, what he famously calls the 'construct' system. Similarity in outlook is therefore very much the engine for rapprochement according to Kelly.

Other commentators have reached similar conclusions using empirical evidence. Griffitt and Veitch of Bowling Green State University for example paid 13 males to spend ten days in a fallout shelter, finding that those with similar attitudes and opinions liked each other most by the end of the study, particularly if they agreed on highly salient issues (Gross, 1991). In the same way, Steve Duck of the University of Iowa found an increased likelihood for mutual liking in people who used similar cognitive constructs (Gross, 1991). In a third study, this time from the UK, Kirton and McCarthy (1988) found that people worked well in environments in which their own cognitive patterns are matched by those around them, what they term 'cognitive fit'. Therefore, according to these three, if the personalities and personal constructs of those interacting are *alike* then the relationship is more likely to prosper than where personalities are dissimilar. In other words, to use popular language, these researchers believe that 'like attracts like'.

This is not to deny the evidence for the opposite view, namely that successful social encounters are defined by difference. However, despite presenting evidence for this engine of attraction, the author of a 'classic' psychology textbook now in its fifth edition, Richard Gross (1991), emphasises the weight of evidence backing up the previously mentioned similarities hypothesis. Likewise, a psychology textbook by Rubin and McNeil of Brandeis University (1987), now in its fourth edition, argues that although diversity is valuable and enriching, people with fundamentally different approaches to life are unlikely to become friends. As the authors write, 'our friends tend to be people who are similar to us' (Rubin and McNeil, 1987, p. 448) since 'people with fundamentally different approaches to life are unlikely to become best friends' (Rubin and McNeil, 1987, p. 462). It seems therefore that the evidence is more supportive of a finding that people of one type attract those who are similar rather than dissimilar.

This phenomenon of like attracting like, known as the 'homogeneity principle' or 'similarity-attraction paradigm' (Byrne, 1971), can occur in organisations, and studies have highlighted the tendency for this phenomenon to influence recruitment, appraisal and promotion (Schneider, 1987; Dipboye and Macan, 1988; Byrne and Neuman, 1992). Schneider's model shows organisations becoming increasingly homogeneous, not only because individuals are attracted to organisations where they believe they will 'fit in' but also because organisational members are likely to feel comfortable with applicants who are similar and thus are likely to hire new employees who hold similar characteristics (Stockdale and Crosby, 2004). Perceived similarity will also impact retention since employees are more likely to be satisfied and remain with an organisation where they feel that they 'fit in'.

Underlying the occurrence of the homogeneity principle is people's use of 'self-reference criteria', those criteria that mirror individuals' use of their own perceptions and choice criteria, a process that is frequently unconscious. So, people may not be aware that they are using 'self-reference criteria' or, as Peter Souter, chairman and chief creative officer of TBWA London and former executive creative director of Abbott Mead Vickers BBDO, has said, that they are 'slightly guilty of hiring themselves' (Moss, 2009, p. 204). Souter works in the world of advertising and the focus of this chapter is the relationship of aesthetic preferences to the personality of the creator and observer. The key question addressed in this chapter is whether aesthetic preferences are more likely to follow a 'like attracts like' or 'opposite attracts' pattern, a question addressed theoretically and empirically.

Aesthetic preferences and personality

Where theoretical literature is concerned, scholar and art critic Joan Evans wrote in *Taste and Temperament* (1939) that 'men of each psychological type tend to admire the art produced by artists of the same type' (1939, p. 47). She went on to suggest that 'A man will always tend to have a primary attraction towards the art produced by men of like temperament with himself' (1939, p. 64). Evans attended St Hugh's College, Oxford, from 1914, graduating in archaeology, and was elected the first woman president of the Society of Antiquaries in 1959, holding the post until 1964. This was something of a family affair, since both her father, Sir John Evans, and her half-brother by more than 40 years, Sir Arthur Evans, best known as the excavator of the Bronze Age archaeological site of Knossos, had also held the post.

Where empirical work is concerned, there has been a very small number of studies examining the link between personality and graphic *preferences*, and using the knowledge presented in Chapter 2 on links between personality and graphic *creations*, we can make some inferences as to whether the artefacts for which people express a preference tend to be the creations of people of *like* type or of *opposite* type to themselves. The studies on personality and graphic preferences were conducted at a similar period to the studies on personality and graphic creations, starting in the late 1940s and coming to a halt in the 1980s. If personality is assumed to be something that can be measured at a single point in time (Hampson, 2000) and if the methodologies of the studies on personality and graphic preferences are taken to be sound, then information on personality and preference can be balanced with information on personality and creations to form a preliminary view as to whether people's visual preferences follow a 'like attracts like' or an 'opposites attract' pattern. This would be the first time, in the author's knowledge, that this question would have been addressed.

So, in the section that follows, information is presented on personality and aesthetic preferences and this is then related to the earlier information presented on personality and graphic expression. It is important to note that although the studies presented were conducted with drawings and paintings, findings in these areas should, theoretically, be transferrable to other graphic disciplines given the consistency of graphic expression across visual disciplines (see Chapter 2). Of course, allowance would need to be made for external factors and constraints (e.g. relating to brands) that may have an influence on creations and preferences.

Empirical studies on preferences and personality

There are nine studies that examine the link between personality and graphic preferences, and in each case, short details of the main findings are related to studies on the personalities associated with particular types of graphic expression.

A. Welsh

Welsh (1949) found that conservative and conventional personalities had a preference for simple and symmetrical objects, while antisocial/dissident personalities had a preference for complex, asymmetrical pictures.

Direction of preferences. Waehner (1946) associated the production of symmetrical drawing with a conventional personality, and the preference conservative types are said to have for symmetrical objects provides an instance of 'like attracting like'. Regrettably, Waehner did not comment on the personality likely to produce asymmetrical images but if it is the converse to 'conventional', then Welsh's view as to the dissident personality's preference for asymmetrical images provides a further instance of 'like attracting like'.

B. Honkavaara

Honkavaara (1958) investigated the relationship between a person's emotional state and his or her pictorial preferences, finding that 'form reactors' (defined as those who are realistic, socially secure, conforming and realistic) demonstrate a preference for 'realistic' pictures, while 'colour reactors' (defined as those who internalise their feelings, are irrational, affectionate and individualistic) evince a preference for 'poetic' pictures.

Direction of preferences. Alschuler and Hattwick (1947) found that those concerned with external stimuli emphasise form above colour while those with stronger emotional drives emphasise colour above form. If it is assumed that the 'realistic' pictures emphasise form above colour, then the form reactors' preference for 'realistic' pictures would appear to instance a 'like attracts like' tendency. In a similar way, the colour reactors' preference for 'poetic' pictures, presumably an expression of an emotional personality, is also likely to be a further manifestation of this tendency. Having said that, we need to bear in mind the limitations of Alschuler and Hattwick's methodologies in asserting this conclusion.

C. Knapp and Green

Knapp and Green (1960) created an abstract art test, finding a preference for clear geometric principles among Extraverted types and a preference for fewer geometric principles among Introverted types.

Direction of preferences. Since Herbert Read (1958) associates the production of geometric forms with intuitive extraverts, Knapp and Green's findings may be a further instance of the 'like attracts like' tendency. The limitations of Read's methodologies, however, reduce the certainty of this finding.

D. Barron

Barron (1963) identified aesthetic preferences of 'responsible, serious' types and those of a more 'emotional and temperamental' disposition with his results presented in Table 6.1.

Direction of preferences. Waehner (1946) interpreted the painting of realistic paintings and landscapes as a sign of conventionality and since Barron (1963) finds that these are the types of paintings preferred by those with 'conservative' personalities, there would appear to be

Table 6.1 Aesthetic preferences associated with particular personality features (Barron, 1963).

Personality characteristics of subjects	Type of paintings preferred
Conservative, serious, deliberate, responsible	Portraits, landscapes and traditional themes
More emotional, temperamental and pessimistic	Experimental, sensual and primitive work

a correspondence between the personality of the beholder and the painter whose work the beholder likes. This, then, is an instance of 'like attracting like'.

E. Knapp and Wolff

Knapp, this time with Wolff (1963), found a preference for abstract art among Intuitive types and a preference for representational art among Sensing types.

Direction of preferences. Herbert Read (1958) and Burt (1968) associate the creation of abstract and representational art with Intuitive and Sensing types respectively, and so Knapp and Wolff's study offers a further instance of a 'like attracts like' tendency.

F. Knapp

In a further study, Knapp (1964) administered the Myers-Briggs Type Indicator (MBTI), finding that

> Preferences for realistic paintings were associated with Extraverted and Sensing types.
> Preferences for geometric paintings were associated with Thinking and Judging types.
> Preferences for expressionist paintings were associated with Introverted and Intuitive types.

Direction of preferences. Since the production of 'realistic' pictures is associated by Read (1958) with Extraverted and Sensing types, and since Knapp's findings are that Extraverted and Sensing types prefer realistic paintings, this appears to be an instance of 'like attracts like'. Moreover, since the creation of 'expressionistic' paintings (a subjective view of reality) is associated by Read with Introverted types, and since Knapp's findings are that Introverted types prefer expressionist paintings, this would appear to be a further instance of 'like attracting like'. The methodological limitations of Read's work do, however, need to be borne in mind.

G. Jacoby

Jacob Jacoby (1969) showed that 'cautious and conservative' individuals favoured small cars while 'confident explorers' favoured large cars. Hammer (1980) and others took the view that large objects are the work of aggressive, confident personalities while small objects are created by those with lesser confidence. If these views are correct, then this study also illustrates the tendency for 'like to attract like'.

H. Birren

Birren (1973), an expert on colour, claimed that colour choices mirror the personalities of those drawn to them, finding that a dislike for colour is associated with difficulties in achieving an agreeable rapport with the outside world as well as introspection and inhibition. By contrast, he claimed that a liking for colour is associated with an agreeable rapport with the outside world as well as emotional responsiveness and outward-directed interests. Birren's claims provide further evidence of a 'like attracts like' basis to people's aesthetic preferences.

I. Eysenck

The British psychologist Hans Eysenck (1981) examined the pictorial preferences of intro-verts and extraverts, finding that introverts showed a preference for old masters over bright, modern pictures, while extraverts showed a reverse pattern. In an earlier study (1941), Eysenck found that extraverts preferred brightly coloured pictures and bright colours to subdued colours.

Direction of preferences. It is not possible to ascertain from Eysenck's later experiment whether this illustrates a 'like attracts like' tendency since there is no data on the link between introversion/extroversion and the creations of 'old masters' and 'bright, modern types of pictures'.

Personality, graphic expression and preferences

A review of the nine studies presented above has shown that in eight cases the characteris-tics of the paintings or colours that people preferred were those associated with the people expressing the preference. This is a preliminary indication that there may be a 'like attracts like' direction or what one might call a 'self-selecting' tendency to people's aesthetic pref-erences, suggesting that people of a particular personality type favour graphic expression originated by those of a similar personality.

This conclusion must remain tentative, however, for while some of the studies correlating personality type to graphic expression had reasonable validity and reliability (e.g. the work of Waehner, 1946), others (e.g. the studies by Read, 1958, and Alschuler and Hattwick, 1947) lacked evidence of such reliability and validity. This means that the evidence for self-selection coming out of studies A and D quoted earlier may be more valid than that emerging from studies B, C, E, F and H.

Having said that, the studies offer sufficient evidence on which to build a working hypothesis that people of a particular type will favour graphic expression mirroring aspects of themselves. In the context of design, it would imply that people respond positively to finished products or graphic design created by those with a similar personality to themselves.

Personality and advertising preferences

What of advertising preferences and personality? Research has shown that the effectiveness of advertisements increases when they use language that is congruent with the personality types of the audience, as measured by the Myers Briggs Type Inventory (MBTI) (McBride, 1988; Yorkston and LaBarbera, 1997), a finding consistent with Buchanan's conclusions (reported in Chapter 7) that website hits increase when the language of the website mir-rors the language typically used by the Myers-Briggs personality types visiting the website. Where visual elements are concerned, one study (LaBarbera et al., 1998) found that colour images believed to be consistent with the sensing/intuitive elements of MBTI types had greatest appeal to those of similar psychological type, regardless of product category.

The next study, using the widely used Big Five personality test, examined the extent to which personality type would influence responses to motivational cues (Hirsh et al., 2012). The study hypothesis was that the effectiveness of a persuasive message was increased when it was congruent with the recipient's personality profile, and this hypothesis was tested by asking 324 subjects, all rated on the Big Five personality test, to rate the effectiveness of a variety of messages about a mobile phone. Each message had been created to respond to the particular motivations of each of the five types.

As hypothesised, extravert subjects valued adverts focused on rewards and social attention; agreeable individuals valued adverts focused on communal goals and interpersonal harmony; conscientious individuals valued adverts focused on achievement, order and efficiency; neurotic individuals valued adverts presenting information about threats and uncertainty while open individuals valued adverts that contained elements of creativity, innovation and intellectual stimulation. In order to illustrate the way in which the language of the message was modified for the hypothesised observer, the advertisement tailored to extraverts included the line 'With XPhone, you'll always be where the excitement is,' while for neurotics, the same line read, 'Stay safe and secure with the XPhone.'

The results across the 324 subjects showed how an advertisement's rated effectiveness could increase with participants' scores on the targeted personality dimension, with responses on all personality types, bar neuroticism, correlating significantly with preferences for the matched advertisement. The authors conclude that manipulating the framing of an appeal to target the Big Five personality traits may provide a useful framework for marketers and that tailoring messages is likely to be more effective than a one-size-fits-all campaign (Noar et al., 2007). In fact, the authors argue that the greater the customisation and adaptation to the unique features of the recipient, the greater is the effectiveness of the tailoring (Dijkstra, 2008). In correlating the reactions of particular personality types to different message cues, this conclusion makes a unique contribution to an assessment of the role of personality in the evaluation of marketing messages. Doing this is all-important given the fact that 'to be successful in today's increasingly competitive marketplace, the appearance of new products has to match the preferences of consumers' (Creusen et al., 2009, pp. 1437–38).

Product design and personality preferences

Where product design is concerned, Govers and Schormans (2005) conducted a study to establish whether certain personalities would be drawn to products that they imagined would have been produced by similar types. The authors claimed to find evidence of product-personality congruence but in fact the study did not measure the personalities of the creators of the products nor of those responding to these. Their findings were based on respondents' assessment of the extent to which the product matched their own personality.

Digital targeting and personality

Recent research on online shopping has shown the extent to which personalisation can be effective in enhancing consumer understanding of product information and purchase intentions (Bosnjak et al., 2007; Woo and Shirmohammadi, 2008; Hirsh et al., 2012). It has also, importantly, looked at the extent to which personality features would influence reactions to online stimuli, examining first the effects of introversion/extroversion and then emotional stability (Nov et al., 2013). Where introversion/extroversion are concerned, the findings from a 53-person study (average age of 28.3) showed that large audience size is associated with an enhanced presence from extraverts and a reduced one from introverts. Low audience size, by contrast, is associated with an increased presence from introverts relative to extraverts.

Where emotional stability is concerned, a concept contrasted with neuroticism, the findings from a 375-person study (average age of 28.7) revealed that emotionally stable personalities are less influenced by social anchors (e.g. ratings of products or services) than neurotic personality types (Arazy et al., 2015). In a further study, the authors examined the impact of conscientiousness on a person's willingness to provide an online rating, finding a correlation between conscientiousness, willingness to rate and negative perception of the number of other people rating (Arazy et al., 2015). The authors highlighted the need for online information to be tailored to the personality or other idiosyncratic personal characteristics so that front-end and back-end design features could respond to user attributes. As they say, 'Once designers are able to profile users based on their personality, they could adapt the interfaces such that users with dissimilar personalities are exposed to different UI features' (Arazy et al., 2015, p. 25). They went on to suggest the need to explore systems where features can be adapted to users' personal attributes – for example in e-learning, where users frequently complete questionnaires and where the completion of a personality questionnaire would not appear idiosyncratic.

Meanwhile Buchanan, whose research is presented in the next chapter (Chapter 7), has shown how the language of websites can be optimised for audiences of different MBTI personality types. As can be seen, ensuring that the website language is adapted to the personalities of those visiting websites can enhance the attractions of those websites for users and increase visitor numbers.

Digital targeting, personality and age

While personality is an important variable, so too is age and a study of these two variables together has impacted the study of digital use among the 50-plus age group (Moss et al., 2013). This older sector of the population has been a focus of study since the majority of those currently in this age group have lived their lives without the Internet (Loges and Jung, 2001, p. 542) and the consequent 'grey digital divide' may disappear as the next generation of 50-plus age groups spends more of their working lives with computers. On the other hand, as Loges and Jung (2001) have pointed out, older people may show a more permanent disposition to preserve their privacy and finances, thereby reducing their propensity relative to younger people to purchase products or services online (Loges and Jung, 2001, p. 559).

Focusing on the current generation of older users in the UK, more than 64% of those over 65 in the UK have never used the Internet (Office for National Statistics [ONS], 2008). Despite continuing growth in the Internet population, ONS reported in 2010 that 18% of all UK adults had not been online (ONS, 2011). Of this group of non-users, 60% consisted of those aged 65 and more and 22% of those aged 55 to 64. Relatedly, research from the Institute for Fiscal Studies (Leicester et al., 2009) commissioned by Age Concern and Help the Aged showed that non-pensioners increased their spending on communications technology at 2.5 times the rate of pensioners over the previous 12 years.

The greater income spent by non-pensioners underlies Timms's prediction (2003) that the digital divide could worsen in the UK before improving. A Library and Information Commission survey revealed in fact a lack of access to computers and the Internet to be a major barrier for older groups (Flatten et al., 2000, p. 11), and a government response to this was the creation of over 6,000 online centres in libraries and elsewhere in the UK (Museums Libraries and Archives Council, 2004). These structural difficulties in access increase the priority for marketers to successfully reach older members of the digital population, ensuring that their time online is effective. To what extent is personality being used as an aid in addressing this group?

A recent UK study (Sudbury and Simcock, 2009) identified five market segments in the UK from a sample of 650 respondents aged 50–79 (mean age 62), these being the *Solitary Sceptics, Bargain-Hunting Belongers, Self-Assured Sociables, Positive Pioneers* and *Cautious Comfortables.* In subsequent work Sudbury and Simcock (2011) identified two of these segments as accounting for over two-thirds of the 'silver market', these being the *Bargain-Hunting Belongers* (38%) and *Positive Pioneers* (30%). Not surprisingly, this led to the proposal for a better understanding of these segments to assist marketers in more effective marketing.

A word on these categories. The *Bargain-Hunting Belongers* are described as the group with the oldest demographic, being 70-plus but with an average self-perceived age of 61 (only 4% still feeling young). They are described as the least affluent segment, with the vast majority now retired. Despite its older age, this group feels healthier than *Solitary Sceptics,* yet, in terms of hobbies and pastimes, they are the least physically active. Their media consumption profile reveals that they are the highest consumers of television, relatively high consumers of radio, newspapers and magazines, but have the lowest Internet usage. Many *Bargain-Hunting Belongers* live alone yet see their friends more frequently than any other segment and are close to their families. They display only relatively positive attitudes towards marketing and consumerism and, on account possibly of restricted incomes, are highly price-conscious, displaying very positive attitudes towards senior discounts. This segment is also less credit-averse than many of the other segments.

The *Positive Pioneers,* on the other hand, are the youngest of the segments in terms of both chronological and cognitive age: a 56-year-old person feels 10 years younger and nobody feels old. Those in this segment are relatively affluent despite having the fewest empty nests, with more than one in four still having grown-up children living at home, and more than half having young grandchildren. Not surprisingly, they also have the most frequent contact with their families of any segment, are active travellers and are not particularly price-conscious. Despite their relatively young age, only half rate their health as good, suggesting the presence of some minor health problems in this segment. More than half enjoy energetic activities, a further third is moderately active, and they take the most vacations abroad of any of the segments. This segment can be accessed through magazines and the Internet, but has the lowest levels of radio consumption.

The smaller segment of the *Cautious Comfortables,* with an average age of 58, feels ten years younger than their chronological age and are the most affluent segment, with 50% of the group still working. They are said to be the healthiest and most energetic of the segments, enjoying, like the *Positive Pioneers,* travel in the UK and abroad. Importantly, they use the Internet more frequently than any of the other segments and have positive attitudes towards advertising and consumerism.

One problematic element to Sudbury and Simcock's classification is the conflation within the categories of chronological and personality features. Where the *Cautious Comfortables* are concerned for example, this group is younger than some of the other groups (e.g. the *Bargain-Hunting Belongers* are older than the other two groups) but also different in psychological type to other groups (e.g. the *Positive Pioneers* and *Cautious Comfortables* are from similar age groups but distinguished on psychological dimensions). So questions then arise as to (a) how marketers could ascertain the personality types of their target markets using Sudbury and Simcock's model and (b) whether the psychological types identified by

Sudbury and Simcock hold true across different age groups. Further research is needed to answer these questions.

Conclusions

The work described in this chapter shows the importance of understanding of the role played by personality in design and advertising *creations* as well as *preferences*. The evidence suggests that the homogeneity principle which powerfully explains social preferences, also explains the processes involved in for design and advertising, with a match between the personality of the creator and that of the end user producing enhanced appeal. Given the existing evidence for this, and the powerful role played by preferences in responses to design and advertising, it is to be hoped that future research will enhance our understanding of the role played by personality in design preferences.

References

Alschuler, R. H. and Hattwick, L. W. (1947). *Painting and Personality.* Chicago: University of Chicago Press.

Arazy, O., Nov, O. and Kumar, N. (2015). Personalityzation: UI personalization, theoretical grounding in HCI and design research. *AIS Transactions on Human-Computer Interaction (AIS THCI)*, 7(2), pp. 43–69.

Barron, F. (1963). *Creativity and Psychological Health.* Princeton, NJ: Van Nostrand Press.

Birren, F. (1973). Colour preference as a clue to personality. *Art Psychotherapy*, 1, pp. 13–16.

Bloch, P. H., Brunel, F. F. and Todd, S. J. (2003). Individual differences in the centrality of visual product aesthetics: Concept and measurement. *Journal of Personality and Social Psychology*, 71, pp. 665–679.

Bosnjak, M., Galesic, M. and Tuten, T. (2007). Personality determinants of online shopping: Explaining online purchase intentions using a hierarchical approach. *Journal of Business Research*, 60(6), pp. 597–605.

Buchanan, R. (1995). Rhetoric, humanism and design, in Buchanan, R. and Margolin, V. (eds), *Discovering Design.* Chicago: University of Chicago Press, pp. 23–68.

Buchanan, R. (2001). Design research and the new learning. *Design Issues*, 17(4), pp. 1–21. http://www.idemployee.id.tue.nl/g.w.m.rauterberg/lecturenotes/DG000%20SCA/buchanan_2001_design_res.pdf [accessed 11 October 2016].

Burt, R. B. (1968). *An Exploratory Study of Personality Manifestations in Paintings.* Doctoral dissertation, Duke University, Dissertation Abstracts International 29, 1493–B Order number 68–14, 298.

Byrne, D. (1971). *The Attraction Paradigm.* New York: Academic Press.

Byrne, D. and Neuman, J. (1992). The implications of attraction research for organizational issues, in Kelley, K. (ed.), *Issues, Theory and Research in Industrial and Organizational Psychology.* New York: Elsevier, pp. 29–70.

Coates, D. (2003). *Watches Tell More Than Time: Product Design, Information and the Quest for Elegance.* New York: McGraw-Hill.

Creusen, M., Veryzer, R. and Schoormans, J. (2010). Product value importance and consumer preference for visual complexity and symmetry. *European Journal of Marketing*, 49(9/10), pp. 1437–1452.

Dell'Era, C., Marchesi, A. and Verganti, R. (2010). Mastering technologies in design-driven innovations: How two Italian furniture companies make design a central part of their innovation process. *Research Technology Management*, 53(2), pp. 12–23.

Dijkstra, A. (2008). The psychology of tailoring-ingredients in computer-tailored persuasion. *Social and Personality Psychology Compass*, 2, pp. 765–784.

Dipboye, R. and Macan, T. (1988). A process view of the selection/recruitment interview, in Schuler, R., Youngblood, S. A. and Huber, V. L. (eds), *Readings in Personnel and Human Resource Management*. St Paul, MN: West.

e-Marketer (2014). Global ad spending growth to double this year. http://www.emarketer.com/Article/Global-Ad-Spending-Growth-Double-This-Year/1010997 [accessed on 1 January 2015].

Evans, J. (1939). *Taste and Temperament*. London: Jonathan Cape.

Eysenck, H. J. (1941). A critical and experimental study of color preferences. *American Journal of Psychology*, 54, pp. 385–394.

Eysenck, H. J. (1981). Aesthetic preferences and individual differences, in O'Hare, D. (ed), *Psychology and the Arts*. Brighton: Harvester Press, pp. 76–101.

Flatten, K., Haddock, S., Clarkson, T. and Bradford, S. (2000). Internet access for older adults in public libraries. Library and Information Commission Research Report 50.

Gehrt, K. and Yan, R.-N. (2004). Situational, consumer, and retailer factors affecting Internet, catalog, and store shopping. *International Journal of Retail and Distribution Management*, 32(1), pp. 5–18.

Govers, P. and Schormans, J. (2005). Product personality and its influence on consumer preference. *Journal of Consumer Marketing*, 22(4), pp. 189–197.

Gross, R. D. (1991). *The Science of Mind and Behaviour*. London: Hodder and Stoughton.

Hammer, M. (1995). *Reengineering the Corporation*. London: Nicholas Brearley.

Hammer, E. F. (1980). *The Clinical Application of Projective Drawings*. Springfield: Charles C. Thomas.

Hampson, E. (2000). Sexual differentiation of spatial functions in humans. In Matsumoto, A. (ed), *Sexual Differentiation of the Brain*. London, UK: CRC Press, pp. 279–300.

Hassenzahl, M. (2007). Aesthetics in interactive products: Correlates and consequences of beauty. In Schifferstein, H.N.J. and Hekkert, P. (eds), *Product Experience*. Amsterdam: Elsevier, pp. 287–302.

Hirsh, J. B., Kang, S. K. and Bodenhausen, G. V. (2012). Personalized persuasion tailoring persuasive appeals to recipients' personality traits. *Psychological Science*, 23(6), pp. 578–581.

Honkavaara, S. (1958). The relationship of interpersonal preference and emotional attitudes of the subjects. *Journal of Psychology*, 46, pp. 25–31.

Jacoby, J. (1969). Personality and consumer behaviour, how not to find relationships. *Purdue Papers in Consumer Psychology*, 102. Lafayette, IN: Purdue University.

Karande, K., Zinkhan, G. M. and Lum, A. B. (1997). Brand Personality and Self-concept: A Replication and Extension. *American Marketing Association, Summer Conference*, pp. 165–171.

Kelly, G. (1955). *The Psychology of Personal Constructs*. New York: W.W. Norton.

Kirton, M. J. and McCarthy, R. M. (1988). Cognitive climate and organisations. *Journal of Occupational Psychology*, 61, pp. 175–184.

Knapp, R. H. (1964). An experimental study of a triadic hypothesis concerning the sources of aesthetic imagery. *Journal of Projective Techniques and Personality Assessment*, 28, pp. 49–54.

Knapp, R. H. and Green, S. M. (1960). Preferences for styles of abstract art and their personality correlates. *Journal of Projective Techniques and Personality Assessment*, 24, pp. 396–402.

Knapp, R. H. and Wolff, A. (1963). Preferences for abstract and representational art. *Journal of Social Psychology*, 60, pp. 255–262.

LaBarbera, P., Weingard, P. and Yorkston, E. (1998). Matching the message to the mind: Advertising imagery and consumer processing styles. *Journal of Advertising Research*, 38(5), pp. 29–43.

Lawson, B. (1983). *How Designers Think*. Westfield, NJ: Eastview Editions.

Leicester, A., O'Dea, C. and Oldfield, Z. (2009). 'Institute for Fiscal Studies'. In: *The Expenditure Experience of Older Households*, Institute for Fiscal Studies Commentary 111. http://www.ifs.org.uk/comms/comm111.pdf [accessed August 15, 2012].

Loges, W. E. and Jung, J.-Y. (2001). Exploring the digital divide: Internet connectedness and age. *Communication Research*, 28(4), pp. 536–562.

Maeda, J. (2006). *The Laws of Simplicity*. Cambridge, MA: MIT Press.

Maughan, L., Gutnikov, S. and Stevens, R. (2007). Like more, look more: Look more, like more: The evidence from eye-tracking. *Journal of Brand Management*, 14(4), pp. 336–343.

McBride, M. (1988). The Theory of Psychological Type Congruence for Advertisers Revisited, *Atlantic Marketing Association*, 4th Annual Conference.

Mischel, W. (1997). The interaction of person and situation, in Magnusson, D. and Endler, N. S. (eds), *Personality at the Crossroads: Current Issues in Interactional Psychology*. Hillsdale, NJ: Erlbaum, pp. 333–352.

Moss, G. (2009). *Gender, Design and Marketing*. Farnham: Gower.

Moss, G., Wulf, C. and Mullen, H. (2013). Internet marketing to 50+ generations in the UK and France. *Journal of International Consumer Marketing*, 25, pp. 45–58.

Museums Libraries and Archives Council. (2004). *The People's Network*. http://www.peoples-network.gov.uk/ [accessed July 27, 2012].

Nielsen, J. (2001). *113 Design Guidelines for Homepage Usability*. http://www.useit.com/homepageusability/guidelines.html [accessed 3 April 2012].

Nixon, S. (1997). Circulating culture, in Gay, P. du (ed), *Production of Culture/Cultures of Production*. London: SAGE, pp. 177–234.

Noar, S. M., Benac, C. N. and Harris, M. S. (2007). Does tailoring matter? Meta-analytic review of tailored print health behaviour change interventions. *Psychological Bulletin*, 133, pp. 673–693.

Noble, C. H. and Kumar, M. (2010). Exploring the appeal of product design: A grounded, value-based model of key design elements and relationships. *Journal of Product Innovation Management*, 27(5), pp. 640–657.

Norman, D. (2004). *Emotional Design: Why We Love or Hate Everyday Things*. New York: Basic Books.

Nov, O., Arazy, O., Lopez, C. and Brusilovsky, P. (2013). Exploring Personality-targeted UI Design in Online Social Participation Systems, *Proceedings of the ACM Conference on Human Factors in Computing Systems (CHI 2013)*. Paris, France.

Office for National Statistics. (2008). http://www.ons.gov.uk/ons/rel/population-trends-rd/population-trends/index.html [accessed December 30, 2012].

Office for National Statistics. (2011). *Internet Access – Households and Individuals (2011)*. http://www.ons.gov.uk/ons/rel/rdit2/internet-access–households-and-individuals/2011/stb-internet-access-2011.html#tab-Key-points [accessed June 19, 2012].

Read, H. (1958). *Education through Art*. London: Faber and Faber.

Rubin, Z. and McNeil, E. (1987). *Psychology of Being Human*. 4th edition, London: HarperCollins.

Schmitt, B. H. and Simonson, A. (1997). *Marketing Aesthetics: The Strategic Management of Brands, Identity and Image*. New York: The Free Press.

Schneider, B. (1987). The people make the place. *Personnel Psychology*, 40, pp. 437–353.

Stockdale, M. and Crosby, F. (2004). *The Psychology and Management of Workplace Diversity*. Malden, MA: Blackwell.

Sudbury, L. and Simcock, P. (2009). Understanding older consumers through cognitive age and the list of values: A UK-based perspective. *Psychology and Marketing*, 26(1), pp. 22–38.

Sudbury, L. and Simcock, P. (2011). Bargain hunting belongers and positive pioneers: Key silver market segments in the UK, in Kohlbacher, F. and Herstatt, C. (eds), *The Silver Market Phenomenon: Marketing and Innovation in the Aging Society*. London: Springer, pp. 195–202.

Timms, D. (2003). New media: How will the other half live? *The Guardian*, 3 November, p. 38.

Van der Heijden, H. (2003). Factors influencing the usage of websites: The case of a generic portal in the Netherlands. *Information Management*, 40(6), pp. 541–549.

Van Iwaarden, J., van der Wiele, T., Ball, L. and Millen, R. (2004). Perceptions about the quality of web sites: A survey amongst students at Northeaster University and Erasmus University. *Information and Management*, 41(8), pp. 947–959.

Veryzer, R. (1993). Aesthetic response and the influence of design principles on product preferences. *Advances in Consumer Research*, 20, pp. 224–228.

Waehner, T. S. (1946). Interpretations of spontaneous drawings and paintings. *Genetic Psychology Monograph*, 33, pp. 3–70.

Welsh, G. S. (1949). *A Projective Test for Diagnosis of Psychopathology*. Unpublished PhD thesis, University of Minnesota.

Woo, N. H. and Shirmohammadi, S. (2008). Modelling and Measurement of Personality for E-commerce Systems, Instrumentation and Measurement Technology Conference Proceedings. IEEE, pp. 787–792.

Yorkston, E. A. and LaBarbera, P. A. (1997). Personality-related Cognitive Style and Advertising Strategy. New and Evolving Paradigms: The Emerging Future of Marketing. Chicago: AMA Conference Proceedings, pp. 802–814.

Chapter 7

Matching communication styles to the personality of web visitors

Holly Buchanan

Introduction

Rule number one in copywriting is to write for the audience (Cornelissen, 2000). It is important to know demographics, psychographics and more specifically what buying process and communication style an audience prefers when shopping for a product or service. The problem is that not all of an audience will have the same preferences. The challenge becomes: how to establish the different preferences, and determine which predominate?

It is important to have a framework with which to segment different audience preferences. The Myers-Briggs Type Indicator (MBTI) test measures psychological preferences in relation to how people perceive the world and make decisions. There are 16 types, and each type has a preferred buying process and communication style. Not all of an audience will have the same type, but one can infer a preferred buying process and communication style by analysing customer communication.

By understanding and mimicking the audience's preferences, copywriters can create more persuasive communication. Research like the 'theory of congruence' and the 'homogeneity principle' shows people respond to those they perceive to be like themselves and that persuasiveness can be enhanced by creating similarity between source and receiver. This idea is expanded ahead.

To be more effective, copywriters need to be aware of not imposing their own personal type, buying process and communication style when they create messaging (unless their preferred type matches that of the target audience). And using MBTI as a framework, analysis can be conducted to determine audience preferences and which preferences are most predominant. Copywriters can generate better results by mimicking these preferences in order to connect with, and persuade, their audience.

The homogeneity principle

There is much research that supports the theory that we are attracted to those who are like us, including the homogeneity principle. In her book *Gender, Design and Marketing* (2009) Gloria Moss discusses this principle and explains that this principle is one in which a person of one type is attracted to another person of similar type. In a recruitment context, she explains that it is referred to as the 'self-selecting' tendency since it is widely recognised that people tend to prefer other people similar to themselves. People are said to be using 'self-reference criteria' – the use of their own perceptions and choice criteria to determine what is important – and sometimes the process of doing this is unconscious. This means that people are often not aware that they are using self-reference criteria and, in the context of evaluations of communications, may not appreciate that the value of a piece of communications is not absolute but is the product of empathy between object, perceiver and artist. Instead, they make the mistake of assuming that the criteria they employ are applied universally.

Moss notes that there is some awareness that it may be less than optimum to use universal criteria of excellence. For example the business guru Michael Hammer, father of the concept of 'business reengineering', spoke of the need for products to be shaped around the 'unique and particular needs' of the customer (Hammer, 1995, p. 21), and for products and services to be 'configured to' the needs of customers (Hammer, 1995, p. 21). In the field of branding, similarly, academics Karande, Zinkhan and Lum have expressed the view that there should be congruence between the brand personality and the consumer's self-concept on the basis that purchases are thought to offer a vehicle for self-expression (Karande et al., 1997). This has led to a search for an understanding of the factors that influence congruence.

Moreover, in my own field, that of communications, it has translated into the notion that persuasiveness can be enhanced by similarity between source and receiver (Brock, 1965). In social psychology, it translates into the 'matching hypothesis' or 'similarity-attraction' paradigm, according to which increased similarity leads to increased attention and attraction (Byrne and Nelson, 1965; Berscied and Walster, 1978). In other words, the person you like is the person who mirrors your own thoughts and views, and this person may possibly even mirror your looks and behaviour.

Findings continue to emerge about the importance of congruence (or 'rapport' or 'mirroring' as it is sometimes called). At California State University, Sacramento, a study of psychotherapists' successes with their clients showed that those therapists who achieved the best results had the most emotional congruence with their patients at meaningful junctures in the therapy. These mirroring behaviours showed up simultaneously as the therapists comfortably settled into the climate of their clients' worlds by establishing good rapport. When reporting these effects, psychiatrist Dr Louann Brizendine referred to 'mirror neurons' that allow people (mainly women in fact) not only to observe but also to imitate or mirror the hand gestures, body postures, breathing rates, gazes and facial expressions of other people (Brizendine, 2006).

If this emotional mirroring can give psychotherapists the edge, it may do the same for communications specialists. The congruity principle relates to the similarity between source and receiver, and research shows that mirroring the thoughts and views of your audience or interlocutor offers the key to more persuasive communications. The driving force here is to communicate in a style similar to that of the receiver whom you hope to persuade. The important driving force here is to focus on the attributes, benefits and motivations of the person you hope to galvanise into action.

Myers-Briggs personality test instrument

The Myers & Briggs Foundation website describes the Myers-Briggs Type Indicator (MBTI) test and the theory behind it.

The essence of the theory is that much seemingly random variation in behaviour is actually quite orderly and consistent, being due to basic differences in ways individuals prefer to use their perception and judgement.

Perception involves all the ways of becoming aware of things, people, happenings or ideas. Judgement involves all the ways of coming to conclusions about what has been perceived.

If people differ systematically in what they perceive and in how they reach conclusions, then it is only reasonable for them to differ correspondingly in their interests, reactions, values, motivations and skills. MBTI preferences are broken down into four dichotomous personality types, which are described on the Myers & Briggs Foundation website as follows:

> **Favourite world** Do you prefer to focus on the outer world or on your own inner world? This is called Extraversion (E) or Introversion (I). **Information** Do you prefer to focus on the basic information you take in or do you prefer to interpret and add meaning? This is called Sensing (S) or Intuition (N). **Decisions** When making decisions, do you prefer to first look at logic and consistency or first look at the people and special circumstances? This is called Thinking (T) or Feeling (F). **Structure** In dealing with the outside world, do you prefer to get things decided or do you prefer to stay open to new information and options? This is called Judging (J) or Perceiving (P).
>
> (Myers, 1998)

Many studies over the years have proven the validity of the MBTI instrument in three categories: (1) the validity of the four separate preference scales; (2) the validity of the four preference pairs as dichotomies; and (3) the validity of whole types or particular combinations of preferences. Many of these studies are discussed in the *MBTI Manual* (Myers, 1998) and separate studies have demonstrated strong construct validity for the MBTI (Thompson and Borrello, 1986) as well as strong internal consistency and test-retest reliability (Capraro and Capraro, 2002). By using MBTI preferences as a framework, it is possible to look for patterns in customer communication and behaviour to see which preferences customers display.

Methodology

In this research, an online women's clothing company wanted to ensure that the copy on its website was adapted to the preferences of the users of the site. In order to do this, the researcher analysed the language used by those contributing to onsite reviews with a view to identifying the MBTI type of these users and from that – following the homogeneity or congruity principle – identify the style of language that should be used on the website to match this.

The clothing company was Fit Couture (www.fitcouture.com), an online women's workout clothing company targeting women aged 25–49 who were looking for stylish exercise clothes designed specifically for women. When the researcher first started working with this company, one of the owners was doing most of the copywriting. In interactions with him, the researcher judged him to be an NTJ, the MBTI Intuitive, Thinking and Judging type, and corroborative evidence was derived from his copywriting style, which also appeared to reflect this type. The researcher also read hundreds of customer reviews and, following analysis, judged that the preferred communication style was SFP, the Sensing, Feeling and Perceiving type. All these traits are in fact opposite in type to those of the owner/copywriter and so, in order to satisfy the preferences of the end-users, the researcher changed the 'voice' of the website and emails from NTJ to SFP.

Pen portraits of these types are presented ahead so that the reader can appreciate the changes involved in moving from a text appropriate to an NTJ as against an SFP type.

NTJ and SFP overview

NTJs are frank and decisive. They quickly see illogical and inefficient procedures and policies, and develop and implement comprehensive systems to solve organisational problems. They are forceful in presenting their ideas. They are sceptical and independent, and have high standards of competence and performance – for themselves and others.

SFPs are friendly, sensitive and accepting. They enjoy the present moment and focus on what is going on around them. They dislike disagreements and conflicts, and do not force their opinions or values on others. They are exuberant lovers of life, people and material comforts. They are flexible and spontaneous. In terms of communication styles, the differences between an NTJ and an SFP communication and decision-making style are likely to be as follows.

An NTJ:

- Is hierarchical.
- Can be sceptical and critical both of themselves and others.
- Passes strong pronouncements with words like 'should'.
- Uses technical terms.
- Focuses on the big picture and generalities.
- Uses third person.

An SFP:

- Focuses on the senses – the look, feel and smell of a product.
- Seeks harmony and the positive in people.
- Goes with the flow and is generally agreeable.
- Is informal and friendly, using slang and contractions.
- Focuses on specifics.
- Uses first and second person.

When reviewing customer communications, the researcher looked for patterns of word use, product benefits discussed, descriptions of motivations and outcomes, and length of review. She looked for frequency of the different patterns to see which were most predominant. Once the preferred type was determined (SFP), copy was revised to mirror this type.

Sample copy

Here are samples of the original copy written by the NTJ owner compared with the new copy written in the SFP style.

Old copy: Fit Couture is designed to make you look your absolute best. Choose from comfortable clothes with a flattering fit and moisture-wicking fabric.

New copy: You're going to love the way you look in Fit Couture. Go ahead, take a second glance in the mirror. Yup, even your butt looks good. And you can sweat in these clothes with material designed to pull away moisture and keep you dry and comfortable.

Changes: The use of the third person was changed to the second person and the hierarchical language (*looking the best*) was replaced by language focusing on the senses (*how your butt looks, glancing in the mirror*). Technical-sounding words (*moisture-wicking fabric*) were replaced with conversational simple terms (*designed to pull away moisture and keep you dry and comfortable*).

Old copy: Real clothes should look great on real bodies, not just on mannequins and models.

New copy: Our clothes are designed for women by women. They fit and flatter real women's bodies in all their wonderful variety, shapes and sizes.

Changes: The copy, which was judgemental in tone (*should look good, not just on mannequins and models*), was changed to something with a more personal positive feel (*fit and flatter bodies in their wonderful variety of shapes and sizes*).

Old copy: No matter how fabulous that outfit looked in the store, if it doesn't make you look great, it doesn't deserve a place in your closet.

New copy: Make room in your closet. Women love Fit Couture pants and clothing so much they often buy three, four, even five pairs. When clothes look and feel this good, why wear anything else?

Changes: Changed critical bias (*if it doesn't make you look great, it doesn't deserve a place in your closet*) to a positive action (*make room in your closet*). Added specific numbers (*three, four, even five pairs*).

Old copy: Some days it feels like you live in your active wear: from gym to shopping to picking up the kids. Changing clothes for every stop is just not an option. Neither is that threadbare pair of sweats and t-shirt in your drawer.

New copy: Fit Couture's stylish, comfortable clothes have a split personality – equally at home in the gym as they are outside of the gym. From yoga to grocery shopping to lunch at the neighborhood bistro – just throw on Fit Couture and your favorite lip gloss and you're ready to take on the world.

Changes: The critical bias (*changing clothes . . . not an option. Neither is*) and judgemental verbiage (*threadbare . . . sweats*) was amended to having a more positive bias with second person (*you're ready to take on the world*). Also added specifics (*lunch at the neighborhood bistro . . . lip gloss*).

Old copy: We're not all the same height, so why should our pants all be the same length? Fit Couture's pants come in lengths ranging from petite to extra long.

New copy: Finally, workout pants that are the right length! Fit Couture's pants come in lengths ranging from petite to extra long. That's right, pick your size, *then* choose the length. No bare ankles, no hemming. How cool is that?

Changes: The word 'should' was changed to a verb with a more positive angle. Moreover, specifics were added (*no bare ankles, no hemming*) and a more informal and conversational tone (*How cool is that?*) was adopted.

Results

In an A/B email test, one version was written in the old style (NTJ), one version was written in the new style (SFP) and the new style (SFP) achieved a 27% higher click-through rate. The client was convinced that the new copy was effective and made changes throughout the site.

Conclusion

The homogeneity and congruency principle demonstrates the importance of similarity between source and receiver in order for a message to be persuasive. Therefore, it is important to analyse customer communications to discern the customer's preferred buying process, personality type and communication style. Once that pattern has been inferred, it is possible to mirror those qualities back to the customer.

With the Internet this analysis is now a much simpler process. Companies and copywriters can review customer emails, live chats and product reviews, and the MBTI can be used as a framework to look for patterns and preferences. All messaging should be reviewed and tested to make sure it is persuasive not just to the creator(s) (the copywriter, advertising agency, business owner) but also to the intended audience.

References

Berscied, E. and Walster, E. (1978). *Interpersonal Attraction*. Cambridge, MA: Cambridge University Press.

Brizendine, L. (2006). *The Female Brain*. New York: Morgan Road Books.

Brock, T. C. (1965). Communicator-recipient similarity and decision change. *Journal of Personality and Social Psychology*, 1, pp. 650–654.

Byrne, D. and Nelson, D. (1965). Attraction as a linear function of positive reinforcement. *Journal of Personality and Social Psychology*, 1, pp. 659–663.

Capraro, R. M. and Capraro, M. M. (2002). Myers-Briggs Type Indicator score reliability across studies: A meta-analytic reliability generalization study. *Educational and Psychological Measurement*, 92, pp. 590–602.

Cornelissen, J. (2000). Corporate image: An audience centred model. *Corporate Communications: An International Journal*, 5(2), pp. 119–125.

Hammer, M. (1995). *Reengineering the Corporation*. London: Nicholas Brearley.

Karande, K., Zinkhan, G. M. and Lum, A. B. (1997). Brand Personality and Self-concept: A Replication and Extension. American Marketing Association, Summer Conference, pp. 165–171.

Moss, G. (2009). *Gender, Design and Marketing: How Gender Drives Our Perception of Design and Marketing*. Farnham: Gower.

Myers, I. B. (1998). *MBTI Manual: A Guide to the Development and Use of the Myers-Briggs Type Indicator*. Consulting Psychologists Press, Inc. Myers & Briggs Foundation website, http://www.myersbriggs.org/my-mbtipersonality-type/mbti-basics/, accessed on 22 November 2011.

Thompson, B. and Borrello, G. M. (1986). Construct validity of the Myers-Briggs type indicator. *Educational and Psychological Measurement*, 46, pp. 745–752.

Chapter 8

Matching website and audience personalities

The case of music artist marketing

Paul Springer

Introduction: personality and popular music artists' websites

At the beginning of this part of the book, in Chapter 6, Gloria Moss appraised the impact of personality and user preference for design and advertising environments. Moss traced ways that personality and personal expression were understood in the creation of goods and communications and in the reaction of consumers, where she found evidence of congruity between the personality of the stimulus creators and the personality of the observer(s) in positive preferences.

This chapter follows on logically from this earlier chapter by demonstrating the role that personality plays in drawing certain groups to visit music artists' commercial websites. It does this through analysis of two commercial websites, how key visitors (or 'followers') are targeted by commercial agents for specific web spaces, and then retained in those spaces by content that is relevant to their tastes, values and modes of conversation. This mechanism is known as 'pull-marketing' or 'retargeting', to use the language of the advertising technology (adTech) industry.

The two web spaces examined consider the extent of congruity between the personality of the artists and that of online followers, with the latter gauged through the co-opted input of site visitors. It is contended that congruity is reinforced through the active participation of followers and fans who reinforce the values, aesthetic sensibilities and tones of voice already operating in the websites. The cases presented show how followers' cogeneration and spreading of artists communications reinforce the personalities of the site and the artists represented there.

The type of marketing and advertising activity described in this chapter tends to be labelled as 'neuromarketing' (Steidl, 2012), a process that draws on large data sets from social networks and web link recommendations forwarded through one-to-one email, what specialist adTech firm RadiumOne terms 'dark social' (Tpoll, 2014, p. 7). The processes described in respect of the two cases examined in this chapter illustrate the force of the homogeneity principle (described earlier in the book by Moss), where a person ('x') of one type is attracted to another person ('y') of similar type. In this case, person 'x' is the community of people that follow the musician or band, person(s) 'y'. The musician or band personality is shaped through personal inputs to online media by the artist(s) (persons 'y') as well as by a community of followers (persons 'x'), who maintain a continuous flow of updated content in their image. It is argued here that the continuous sharing and readaption of original messages reinforce the personal characteristics of the artists, the community and the individuals reflected within it, in a manner that is unique to the particular community of self-opted followers. Followers can reaffirm 'house' values of the site and further iterate the environment that they would pay a premium to belong to (Hassenzahl, 2007, p. 293).

Case 1: One Direction

At their peak of popularity in May 2014, the pop brand One Direction announced an 'On the Road Again' 2015 tour to promote their new studio album. The first seven (of 80) shows were scheduled for Australia, in a tour that spanned 22 countries over an eight-month period. The first stage of the tour was considered critical by their record label, Syco, in rais-ing awareness and anticipation of the tour dates across the world. To fill venues around the world, the first concerts needed to generate high levels of demand, particularly via their potentially massive volume of core followers, whose word-of-mouth sharing of branded communications through friend networks offline and on social media had the capacity to make the Australian tour a big event and highly relevant.

The challenge for the neurosocial marketing and audience research agency Nine Live was to ensure that all venues sold out in Australia and that the ripple of publicity flowed into the personally shared content of One Direction's fans. Although the record label amassed data on primary adopters from official One Direction subscription sites, these primary adopters would not necessarily share the band's content since many were discreet and were reluctant to share the privileged access to content that they enjoyed.

It should be noted that when tickets went on sale, Nine Live used the data it held on online social habits to segment and re-target relevant audiences during the first wave of orchestrated groundswell activity. The tickets for the first seven concerts were sold within hours of becoming available. A second promotion push when One Direction's album was released (early November 2014) stimulated a huge volume of articles and social content sharing, which, with unique band information, was fed to selected active followers. Sharing activity then caused a reverberating spike in concert bookings and more global awareness in late November, which was rebooted by personal appearances when the band arrived in Australia to perform at the Aria Awards. Increases in social sharing behaviour in networks correlated directly with a spike in sales. Further exclusive information drips to active One Direction site users stimulated ticket transactions and content sharing, and this increased steadily throughout the year leading up to their February 2015 tour.

RadiumOne had provided Nine Live with data from which prospective 'super-fans' could be identified from a data set of 900 million monthly online users, all of whom had shared content relating to One Direction, band members or related pop groups. RadiumOne made particular use of information gleaned from their short URL 'Po.st' link, positioned at the end of news articles, which sharers used as the vehicle for forwarding information to family or friends. RadiumOne also extracted information from an social sharing survey that it con-ducted with data analysts Tpoll in 2014, with responses drawn from over 9,000 consumers in the UK, North America, Europe, Australia and France. In this survey they found that:

- Eighty-four per cent of people share content online globally;
- Thirty-two per cent of people who share content online will share only via email and other closed-access one-to-one channels (termed 'dark social' by marketers); 69% of all sharing activity takes place via dark social globally, compared to 23% via Facebook;
- Thirty-six percent of personalised one-to-one sharing of content with close friends takes place on mobile devices globally (Tpoll, 2014, p. 3).

In terms of activities, One Direction's tour campaign was publicised on official websites as well as on social media forums created by the band and its team. In terms of social media, information was released in waves on Twitter, where it ran through a series of hashtags, primarily #1Dontheroadagain and the central fan streams @onedirection, which had 28.8 million followers at its peak (with 9,830 tweets and 1,596 photo and video shares), as well as @1DFamily (1.26 million followers). This last stream was a primary channel for breaking information, while Instagram became the main repository for images of the group taken by band members and its close entourage. Instagram site One Direction News (@1d.legendary. updates) attracted close to 90,000 followers and 70,000 posts at the time of the concert, and content badged as official on the One Direction site attracted close to 14 million followers for over 500 posts. Facebook became the main repository for new images of One Direction. Its official Facebook and tour site 'On the Road Again' received over 21,000 active messengers involving sharing of reminiscences together with images of the concerts, in total attracting 39 million Facebook likes.

In terms of the character of this activity, the website is separate from the social media platforms, with the latter linked much more to the character of the group than to the website itself. For example the official website is very ordered with a mostly monochrome and geometric appearance and black type on white (apart from the reverse white type on black on the banner). Studio shots and direct quotes of the band members take up the full screen space and are set in a grid of equal proportions. Little on the official site appears informal but the main website operates as a landing point and official space from which visitors can reach the One Direction community. This is facilitated by links to the group's Instagram and Twitter streams as well as to the web spaces of individual members. These domains are much more reflective of the idiosyncrasies of the group than of the official website.

The band's messages to their community are in a tone that suggests that they are messaging personal friends. Individual band members' posts are slightly different since they reflect the different personalities that constitute the band, although they all consistently emote warmth and feeling for their audience, often adopting a self-deprecating tone that calls for a reaffirmation of affection. A theme that is relevant to the moment tends to be selected for each post – for example during the tour it was likely to relate to where they were performing that evening – and the posts tend to involve their following in their comments.

Of all their channels, the Twitter stream #1Dontheroadagain most clearly illustrates these characteristics and, through that, the personality of One Direction. The tone of engagement of the group's Twitter stream is very different from that of the group's website since band members tend to post images with vignettes of their lives and messages with emotive responses to situations (whether entertainment news or award ceremonies), embellished with emojis and slang colloquial expressions. By way of example, band member Liam created a post on winning an award (on 23 May 2016) that read, 'Wow. wow wow [sic] so much everyone for the billboard award I don't understand how we even win stuff anymore [one monkey emoji plus two gritted teeth emojis],' which was retweeted 110,000 times by fans. Another band member, Harry, tended not to use emojis but still messaged as if part of the community rather than in front of it: 'Getting back on the road tomorrow. Can't wait to see all of you in Cardiff. All the love.'

In terms of messages from visitors/'followers', these can be found on the #1Dontheroadagain tour site. The messages here mirror, in tone, those provided by the band members on their own site. In fact, as the examples in Table 8.1 illustrate, many of the visitors' messages are retweets of messages and comments from the main One Direction website as well

Table 8.1 Coding: characteristics of #IDontheroadagain' posts (based on a sample of 100 messages collated by the author).

O = Original R = Re-appropriated F = Forward message, unmediated	Message type/example	Hashtag	Word length	Date	Symbols/emojis
O	**Asserting involvement:** day2''''' the best concert ever	#IDontheroadagain	6	24.03.15	!!!!!! :)
O	**Asserting connection** Can't wait to see you guys in Philippines #IDontheroadagain @Harry_Styles @zaynmalik @Louis_Tomlinson @NiallOfficial @Real_Liam_Payne	#IDontheroadagain	8	15.03.15	kissing emoji
O	**Anticipation** Ahhh! Omg so close	#IDontheroadagain; #onedirection	4	08.01.15	Smiley face emoji, confetti, party popper and heart
O	**Demonstrating commitment** Now I just have to wait till September first to see my boys again	#IDontheroadagain; #onedirection	14	01.11.14	!!!, tears emoji, gritted teeth emoji, heart emoji
O	**Personal address** @NiallOfficial Hai Niall, I want to see you in Indonesia	#IDOnTheRoadAgain	9	02.11.14	Emoji heart
O	**Reach-out/self-validation:** I GOT TICKETTTTTTTSSSSSSSSS	#IDontheroadagain; #JOZI #SOWETO #SOCCERCITY	3	28.05.14	!!!!!!!!!!!!!!!
R	**Self-positioning:** @BigConcerts MOMENTS #Idontheroadagain	#IDOnTheRoadAgain	3	21.05.14	–
F	**Reach-out:** "If you're camping out for the #IDOnTheRoadAgain SA shows please let us know using #IDCampOut"-@TessShorten	#IDOnTheRoadAgain; #IDCampOut	15	22.03.15	Emoji smiley face
O	**Dismay:** thinks its a bit unfair only telstra customers can only purchase pre sale tickets for #Idontheroadagain actually really unfairrrr	#IDontheroadagain; #nothappy	20	18.05.14	–
F	@onedirection TICKETS SALES ON FRIDAY 9am MAKE SURE U GET TICKETS!!	#IDontheroadagain	10	19.05.14	–

as from band members' Twitter streams. So for example Liam's tweet noted earlier was retweeted 110,000 times.

What form do followers' messages take? Typically, comments tend to reiterate statements of unbounded excitement for newly announced band activity, with happy expressions composed from the limited repertoire of emojis and affirmative punctuation keyboard characters available on most smartphones – for instance '20 days until I see my one and only's [*sic*] [followed by 11 emojis, including three with hearts and two clapping hands]'. Messages tend also to repeat band news with little information added other than excited expressions. Hashtag message chains are composed largely of half-sentence additions to initial statements, a particularly common occurrence in the case of messages posted from countries not on the band's itinerary. In essence, those who obtained tickets for the concerts emoted excited anticipation while those not able to go were wistful in tone. The consistency of short, emotionally charged messages contrasts with the longer form of sentence found on cause-related sites, such as charities and political organisations. Little factual information other than shared branded content and personal expressions is posted among the many thousands of viewer-generated messages.

How do the messages of the band members compare with those of their followers? As we have seen, band member comments are extravert in character and this appears to be true also of the character of follower comments too since the vast majority of visitors' messages reinforce their shared passion for the band's live performances. This passion on the part of visitors corresponds with that expressed by members of the band, showing a parallel character on the part of the band and of its visitors. Interestingly, the two flows of messages – from the band and from followers – do not run in parallel since band messages are (as we have seen) retweeted by followers and followers' messages are in turn retweeted by the band or by their record label. The personal endorsement of followers' messages by the band makes these messages more shared, and hence more relevant than others. To this extent the band and their agents are curating the flow of relevant messages on band-dedicated social media sites.

A word about the method used for analysing follower comments. A cross section of visitor/follower tweets were selected at regular intervals over a 20-month period, between the dates that the #1Dontheroadagain hashtag launched (February 2014) and the end of the tour (October 2015). The method was based on that used to identify attribute and emotion coding that is commonly conducted for qualitative ontological studies (Saldana, 2012, p. 86). The sample of selected tweets was then reviewed in terms of:

- the origin of the tweet and whether messages are original, re-appropriated from existing messages or forwards of existing content;
- the type of tweets posted and whether the messages demonstrate commitment to the band or appeal to the band's online community;
- the number of words in posted messages;
- typographic characters used – emojis or keyboard symbols (important given the frequent use of emotive shorthand expressions).

From this analysis, various patterns emerged. It was apparent for example that, in terms of shorter messages, those posted *following* key events tended to be simple expressions of praise aimed at the band – 'Can't wait to see you guys in Philippines' [*sic*] – while those posted *prior* to concerts were aimed at the community – 'Ahhh! Omg so close.' In terms of longer messages, these tended to be a call-to-action aimed at the community – for instance

'If you're camping out for the #1DOnTheRoadAgain SA shows please let us know using #1DCampOut.' These longer messages would rally others in the One Direction community to meet and undertake related activities in the margins of the concerts.

The immediacy of personal media, particularly mobile phones, proved to be a winning element for the record label since it was able to drive rapid real-time action by triggering active followers to share breaking band news. Followers appeared to act on impulse given the timing, brevity and immediacy of language used in posts. For example it is noticeable that the first wave of messages from early sharers in the aftermath of new band content tended to consist of retweets of the news tagged quite simply with an emotive expression of joy – most often 'OMG', a smiley emoji or simply '!!!' (between three and ten exclamation marks appeared to be the norm). RadiumOne's data intelligence and Nine Live's management of breaking information stimulated an undercurrent of anticipation through those who sought active participation.

To a large extent, the close correspondence between visitor responses and the mood of the Twitter stream sits neatly with notions of the homogeneity principle described earlier in Chapter 8. The process in the instance of One Direction's network channels is an iterative one in which One Direction's network channels are fed content and followers encouraged to mediate this by applying their own perceptions in order to reaffirm their affinity to the community. This was certainly true of One Direction's Australian fans before and during their initial tour concerts – as Table 8.2 highlights. Ultimately it is the site community of followers that meld the live concerts by One Direction with the perceiver, supporting Karande et al.'s view that there should be congruence between the brand personality and 'the consumer's self-concept with purchases offering a vehicle for self-expression' (Karande et al., 1997, also cited by Moss).

Reflecting more widely, and moving beyond the specific instance of One Direction, it could be said that the need for congruity between brand personality and consumer self-concept mirrors the observations of American anthropologist and fashion writer Ted Polhemus

Table 8.2 What and why Australians share content online (percentage, drawn from a sample of 9,000) (RadiumOne, 2015, p. 5).

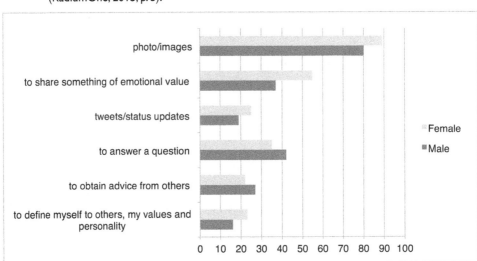

(1996) that self-aware and fashion-conscious teenage consumers tend to adopt popular brands as ready-made identities to communicate their own values, with dress codes and esoteric reference points demonstrating association by proxy. In the same way, comments posted on One Direction's branded website update their authors' affinity to their friends and wider One Direction community.

Context: behind-the-scenes mapping of One Direction's core followers

The agency (RadiumOne) that shaped data on One Direction's core followers gathered data based on viewers' click-throughs to identify the fans most likely to act as ambassadors on the subject's behalf. It employed Dr Peter Steidl, a specialist in neuromarketing, to examine the relationship between sharing online and consumers' emotional state. Steidl focused on how and why Australian youth share content online and discovered that most tended to share immediate key moments of happiness or sadness, especially when related to events. In this way, 89% of women and 80% of men were found to share images to capture a special moment, while 55% of women and 37% of men felt compelled to share something of emotional value (Steidl, 2015, p. 5).

After this, Steidl focused more closely on the sensation of message sharing. He examined the feelings that prospective followers experienced at the point of sharing/receiving stimulating content as well as the motivations that underpinned the sharing of content within their networks. He imagined that 'dopamine' might have a role since this brain chemical stimulates brain and body activity. In particular, dopamine is thought to produce heightened emotional states of desire, driving pleasure-seeking behaviours. As a consequence, the term occurs in the vocabulary of advertisers, and particularly among their consumer planning specialists, to reference the array of motivational factors that prompt people to buy goods or share sales messages. Understanding *why* people become active participants helps marketing practitioners comprehend the steps that need to be taken to apply their data and creativity most purposefully.

Here then is RadiumOne and Steidl's account of the factors influencing consumers' reactions and the role that dopamine plays:

We know that consumers go through a number of phases when:

- They experience a dopamine release which makes them feel good about their sharing initiative;
- Not long afterwards, as the released dopamine dissipates, they will feel a desire for another dopamine hit;
- This makes them more receptive to any proposition they hope might deliver a dopamine release (note that this process takes place in the non-conscious so consumers are typically not aware of why they are more receptive); and;
- If the message we deliver is aligned with the content they shared earlier, we know that they are more open to our offer than consumers who have not shared relevant content.

(Steidl and RadiumOne, 2015, p. 5)

Neuroscientist Mauricio Delgardo and co-authors explicitly relate these processes to communications in the context of social networking, where exchange of information can have the same neurological effect on consumers as offline staples of living, given that 'The same brain areas are activated for food and water [as] for social stimuli' (Balleine et al., 2007, p. 8162).

Music functions similarly, stimulating an emotional response that connects with lifestyle preferences and value systems and leading fans to want to share music with their friends. Agencies such as RadiumOne make the most of such passion points, re-connecting users by reinforcing shared values at key motivational moments. This activity has proven to heighten the scale and reach of a niche community in which artists provide a central, focal point.

Case 2: Ellie Goulding

British pop singer Ellie Goulding works under the Universal Music Group record label, a group that manages a diverse portfolio of artists spanning a wide spectrum of music genres. The label actively supports its artists through public sharing channels, including Facebook, Twitter, Google+, Pinterest, YouTube, Tumblr, Instagram, Snapchat and LinkedIn. Goulding's website, www.elliegoulding.com, is a subscription website centrally managed by Universal, which provides content for example videos, merchandise and tour dates. The appearance of Goulding's website resembles that of an online fashion magazine insofar as it features large publicity shots of the artist overlaid with large type, referencing recent performances, albums, appearances and merchandise (labelled as 'Merch' on the site). On the main elliegoulding.com site large images of the artist are set against a sky blue background with gold type across the banner. Goulding herself produces short posts on her Twitter stream and these messages are mostly short and informative – 'En route to FireFly festival [fire emoji]' or re-appropriated retweets with short acknowledgements – 'Thanks lover'. The tone of her website is extravert in character, with messages short and punchy in style.

In terms of interaction with the main Goulding 'landing site', more opportunities are afforded to visitors/followers for this than is the case with the One Direction site. Thus, although Goulding's website offers limited opportunities for the co-creation of content by followers, it does provide alternative opportunities to engage with the site. For example followers can offer responses to content on the official website (e.g. by posting a message stream at the foot of news releases) and can forward pages via one of the nine links offered to social media. However, the nature of viewers' comments are primarily in response to official events posted rather than as dialogue with the artist herself, although, having said that, followers still send messages from the official site to the artist directly – see Table 8.3.

It should be noted that the links on Goulding's official web pages that enable viewers to post content through their own online sites were created by Universal and RadiumOne with quick-link domains, such as ell.li (Ellie Goulding), designed to simplify viewer sharing. Data on the way that the links are used helps to identify the most active followers of the artist and can lead to their identification as a seed audience for exclusive news and content on Goulding, which the followers would then share with their friend communities. In this way, followers are using the quick links at www.elliegoulding.com as a repository from which to draw and share content while the label is using data from the accrued activity to determine the identity of its best seed audiences.

In terms of the messages posted by visitors to official sites, a reading of these shows the extent to which followers assume that their messages will reach Goulding personally (see the analysis of visitor messages in Table 8.3). As can be seen, comments consist of questions about the tour ('Is there an opening act for tonight?') and direct messages to the artist ('I am excited to see you tomorrow night in Orlando, FL! I absolutely love listening to all

Table 8.3 Coding: characteristics of visitor messages posted on the site www.elliegoulding.com (based on a sample of 100 messages, collated by the author).

O = Original R = Re-appropriated F = Forward message, unmediated	Message type	Typical word length	Days following/ before a key event (typically)	Symbols/ emojis	Instances (from sample of 100 posts)
O	Direct question/request	13	–5	!!!	8
O	Direct praise		1	;), heart	22
O	Concert critique	43	1	:)	11
O	Emoting (*I Love you*)	5	Sporadic	X, !!!	30
O	End-of-tour reflection	13	7	:)	3
R	Reciting song lyrics	40	Sporadic		2
O	Recount meeting artist	25	Sporadic	–	5
O	Praising performance	15	3	:)	14
O	Comment on awards	32	1	:(	2
	On appearance in press	8	2	–	3

your music! I can't wait!!!! :)'), with many of these direct messages being simple variations on the theme of 'I love you Ellie.'

Most messages tend to address the singer as the focal point rather than address the community around her, something found with greater frequency in the messages created in the One Direction channels. In terms of style, most messages on the Goulding channels are short, featured emojis which appear to have a more juvenile than adult character since they appear to be part of a dialogic attempt to reach the artist. The less frequent and more considered posts, usually critiquing concerts or praising performances, stand out from the majority of emotive comments in being longer and less juvenile in character. Their measured and reasoned tone and personality set them apart from the majority of messages.

How does the character of the visitor comments relate to that of the fixed content of the site? According to Carr (2011), the personality trait of the site is one of

> extraversion, agreeableness, and emotional stability facilitate[ing] the development of friendships, and environments that facilitate the development of friendships offer opportunities for meeting with people who have similar attributes, skills and values. These environments may be associated with education, work, leisure, or family activities.
>
> (Carr, 2011, p. 280)

It is interesting to read of the extravert nature of the Goulding site since those visiting the site, as judged by the character of their messages, are thought to be extravert in character. This shows the way in which the site's extravert character attracts individuals with similar personality characteristics. This produces a matching of personalities that appears to create the conditions for (what RadiumOne refer to as) 'passion points', which can in turn create an idealised basis for friendships, removed from the hassle of education, work and family environments that Carr describes. In short, engagement with Golding's web space offers visitors the possibility of co-opting the collective personality and views of the site, as well the views and values associated with Goulding herself. To this extent, there is clear congruence between the brand personality and the consumer's self-concept on the basis that attending gigs and events and buying branded merchandise offer a vehicle for self-expression (Karande et al., 1997).

Underlying the connections experienced between the site and its visitors, according to Steidl (2015), are the biological effects of mirror neurons. As he writes,

> We have 'mirror neurons' that allow us to feel the emotions that other people feel. This is how we can feel the anger, fear, happiness and other emotions delivered by entertainment experiences. Our mirror neurons are more likely to be activated when we are looking at people and content we relate to . . . We also know that the brain is designed to take shortcuts . . . One of these shortcuts is to follow what others are doing. Behavioural economists call this 'social validation': when many consumers engage with or buy something we assume it is worthwhile doing the same, eliminating the need to carefully consider the activity or offer.
>
> (Steidl, 2015, p. 7)

Steidl's assertion of a biological element in the excitement experienced by visitors to sites that mirror their personality is consistent with the 'homogeneity principle' (Stoat, 2015, p. 15) described by Moss in Chapter 8. The excitement that comes from self-selecting a community that shares a core interest is the basis for attraction, driven by a shared motivational perspective. Steidl (2015) provides a further level of explanation in suggesting that social sharing activates the rewards system of the brain, providing a release stimulated by pleasure-seeking activities similar to those triggered by sex, food and exercise (Swann, 1983, p. 46). While those triggers may be physical in nature, the importance for marketing of acting in the "now" is reinforced by RadiumOne's statistic that 34% of sales through social activity occurs within 20 minutes of the sharing event and advertising message being viewed (2015).

Conclusions

Social sharing is more than an indicator of interest or receptiveness insofar as it appears to offer marketers the opportunity to connect with consumers at the point where they experience moments of openness and emotive rather than reasoned response.

It can be seen that once web users have found an online community that appeals to them, they will tend to engage with the website by reaffirming beliefs that drew them to the site in the first place. In the case of the two websites examined, viewers' communities reinforced existing personality types and reaffirmed traits through a continuous use of localised and colloquial communication. A shared and common outlook together with repeated points of reference created a 'shared own world' within these sites. It is worth noting that the most liked and retweeted viewer-generated messages (the ultimate sign of community approval) chimed with the positive tone of artists. Styles of participation and engagement involved updating the frame of reference and redefining what was important at any given moment. This also reaffirmed existing empathies between artist and fan-follower by reinforcing like-minded views.

For members of niche fan communities, producing remarks that swam against the momentum of the sites would be difficult. Not to participate at all would be to miss out. So, for marketing this constant coerced flow of messages is an opportunity to step closer in harnessing the innate preferences of people within like-minded communities.

References

Balleine, B. W., Delgado, M. R. and Hikosaka, O. (2007). The role of dorsal striatum in reward and decision-making. *Journal of Neuroscience*, 27. Washington: J Neurosci, pp. 8159–8160.

Carr, A. (2011). *Positive Psychology: The Science of Happiness and Human Strengths.* Sussex: Routledge.

Hassenzahl, M. (2007). Aesthetics in interactive products: Correlates and consequences of beauty, in Schifferstein, H.N.J. and Hekkert, P. (eds), *Product Experience.* Amsterdam: Elsevier.

Karande, K., Zinkhan, G. M. and Lum, A. B. (1997). *Brand Personality and Self-concept: A Replication and Extension. American Marketing Association, Summer Conference*, pp. 165–171.

Polhemus, T. (1996). *Style Surfing, What to Wear in the 3rd Millennium.* London: Thames & Hudson.

Saldaña, J. (2012). *The Coding Manuel for Qualitative Researchers.* 2nd ed. Los Angeles: SAGE.

Steidl, P. (2012). *Neurobranding* [n.p.]: CreateSpace.

Steidl, P. and RadiumOne. (2015). *Drugs, Data and Tech: Has Marketing Utopia Arrived?* [online] Available at: http://info.radiumone.com/rs/207-XLI-813/images/RadiumOne_Research_Drugs_Data_Tech.pdf [Accessed 17 June 2016].

Stoat, M. (2015). *Social Media Triggers a Dopamine High. Marketing News* [online] American Marketing Association, November. Available at: https://www.ama.org/publications/MarketingNews/Pages/feeding-the-addiction.aspx [Accessed 16 June 2016] pp. 15–16.

Swann, W. (1983). *Self-verification: Bringing Social Reality into Harmony with the Self.* J. Suls & A. Greenwood (Eds.), *Journal of Social Psychology Perspectives*, Vol. 2. Mawah, NJ: Lawrence Erlbaum, pp. 45–50.

Tpoll (2014). *The Light and Dark of Social Sharing*, RadiumOne, October, pp. 7–8 [online]. Available at: http://info.radiumone.com/rs/radiumone/images/RadiumOne_DarkSocial.pdf [Accessed 17 June 2016].

Chapter 9

How organisations can be optimised for personality-sensitive design

Gloria Moss

The principle of congruence

In the chapters on preferences (Chapter 6), we have seen the strength of personality congruence as a principle in design preferences, with people of one personality type showing a tendency to prefer designs created by those of the same personality. In this final chapter, we will lay bare the organisational mechanisms that can facilitate the achievement of congruity between the personality imprint of a designer in a design and the personality of the end user and purchaser. Achieving this congruity is important since, ultimately, consumers' preference for a product will be strongly correlated with the extent to which their own personality is mirrored in that of the design that they observe.

Ensuring that this congruity is achieved turns on a number of management tasks, including recruitment, appraisal and promotion, ensuring that the personality of the assessor does not obstruct the selection of those with a personality that is congruent with that of the consumer but different from that of the assessor. This necessitates an understanding of the factors that militate in favour of recruitment in one's own image (Dipboye and Macan, 1988; Byrne and Neuman, 1992) as well as of the factors that influence congruity between product and customer self-concept (Brock, 1965; Crozier and Greenhalgh, 1992; Hammer, 1995; Karande et al., 1997; Chernatony and Drury, 2004), factors that can lead to enhanced pleasure and purchasing (Groppel, 1993; Donovan et al., 1994; Yahomoto and Lambert, 1994). It also means having a leadership style in place that is inclusive enough to allow different success criteria to come to the fore within an organisation.

The importance of leadership is not in doubt, for according to a report on organisational performance (Page et al., 2006) a wide range of performance measures impact on organisational effectiveness. These include measures of innovation, one of which relates to new products. In addition, it is thought that the management of an organisation will impact on its culture, providing the context in which the organisation's products and designs are created (Bass, 1998; Alimo-Metcalf and Alban-Metcalf, 2005). As a result, the management of an organisation will also influence its products.

Management influence can operate at several levels. The values of brand managers permeate the brand (Schneider, 2001) and senior management is involved either by spearheading new brand values (Driscoll and Hoffman, 2000) or by recruiting those personnel involved who are involved in marketing, design and branding activities (Moss, 2007). Research that I have conducted on leadership has laid bare the extent to which senior management may quite unwittingly impose its own values during the recruitment process, substituting values that are congruent with their own preferences for the official selection criteria laid down in the job specification (Moss and Daunton, 2006). In some cases, these values may in be at odds with those of the customer constituency (Moss, 2007).

Underpinning these priorities is an interactionist perspective that views aesthetic perceptions as a function of individual rather than universal values (Porteous, 1996), a perspective that inspires the search for segmented values. This perspective links, in turn, with the 'empathy principle', according to which aesthetic value is not inherent in objects but is the product of empathy between object, perceiver and artist (Dipboye and Macan, 1988). A focus on interactive rather than universal principles, as implied by Figure 9.1, would in turn necessitate a tolerance for diversity in the workplace.

The model presented in Figure 9.1 suggests that optimal design and marketing solutions are those where the values inherent in them echo those held by the target market. This follows the mirroring principle, according to which the efficacy of tools or messages is maximised by ensuring that they contain features that mirror the preferences of the target market (Hammer, 1980; Janz and Prasarnphanich, 2003; Moss et al., 2008). In order to satisfy this principle, there needs to be a match between the performance elements (management style, products and designs) and the preferences of the end user. Preferences, as we have seen earlier (see Chapter 6), tend to parallel and mirror performance tendencies, with segmentation variables appearing to act on preferences in an analogous way to the way in which they act on performances.

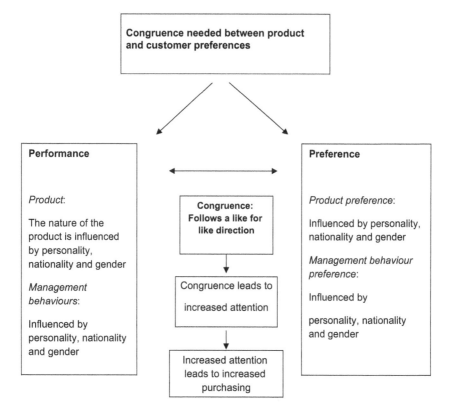

Figure 9.1 Normative model of links that need to exist between performance and preference to create congruence.

The parallels between the psychology of performance on the one hand and the psychology of preference on the other seem to suggest that congruence can best be achieved by ensuring that the people creating products have ways of seeing that are as similar as possible to those of the people consuming products. In other words, where personality is concerned, they suggest that creatives employed by organisations should have personality characteristics that mirror those of the target market. This view is to adopt the 'inside-out' or 'outside-in' perspective (Baden-Fuller, 1995).

We know from data from the Myers-Briggs Type Indicator (MBTI or 'Big Four') that the most common combination of personality types in organisations is ISTJ (Introvert, Sensing, Thinking and Judgement). We also know that up to 83% of purchases are by women (Moss, 2009) and that the relative proportions of 'Thinking' and 'Feeling' types among men and women are not equal, with 65%–76% of women and 33%–45% of men being of the 'Feeling' type (Centre for Applications of Psychological Type, n.d.). In terms of specific occupations, Ashridge data for MBTI in management (Carr et al., 2011) showed that Feeling types are present in 11% of male managers and in 24% of women. This suggests that, since men constitute the majority of managers, the Thinking predisposition will be the dominant type in organisations, leading to a difference in perception between those inside and those outside the organisation. For those not familiar with the Jungian types used in the MBTI, the Thinking/Feeling dimension concerns the extent to which feelings act as an additional factor in decision making, with this being a case with the 'Feeling' type (who can incidentally think logically) and being much less the case with the 'Thinking' type.

In terms of figures showing the male domination of managerial and senior managerial position, this shows a consistent pattern internationally. Thus, in the US, female representation on Fortune 500 company boards remains below 17% for the fourth year running (Catalyst, 2014). In the UK, women hold just 6.1% of executive directorships, up from 5.5% in 2010 (Davies, 2013, p. 6), and across the European Union zone, 15% of non-executive directors and 8.9% of executive directors are women (European Commission, 2012). Internationally, in 2015, in 55% of the 128 countries surveyed by the ILO in 2015, men constituted 70% of managers and leaders, with a higher average demonstrated in the remaining 45% of organisations surveyed (ILO, 2015).

How easy is it to work with a psychological landscape within the organisation that differs from that of the customer base? In a case such as this of a difference in demographic perceptions between those outside and inside an organisation, a paradigm shift is required on the part of an organisation's thinking, necessitating 'transformational' change. This type of change offers a bigger step change than its alternative of 'realignment', which offers no paradigmatic change (Balogun and Hope Hailey, 2008). Transformational change, by contrast, involves more fundamental change and the organisation can choose to do this in a more or less gradual way, with the slow type of change known as 'evolution' and the faster one known as 'revolution' (ibid.).

Practical steps to congruence between internal and external customer preferences

In essence, the radical options involve recruiting and promoting staff whose perceptions and aesthetic preferences match those of the target market. A less radical and more evolutionary strategy would use training to bring about greater diversity in people's thinking, with a programme focused on the diverse nature of aesthetic preferences and possible differences between the thinking of customers on the one hand and the thinking of those in the design and marketing functions on the other.

The first option, that of recruitment, appears, on the face of it, to be the most direct method of achieving congruity with customer perspectives, but regrettably, it is not an obstacle-free option. Firstly, it may be difficult, even using personality testing tools, to find the staff with a personality profile to match that of customers. Secondly, recruiting staff whose values may differ from those of the majority in an organisation may lead to the recruitment of people whose values are at odds with those of the organisational culture, making it difficult for these people to flourish and be valued. Moreover, since people tend to recruit people like themselves (Lewis, 2006), succeeding in breaking out from organisational recruitment norms can be difficult.

In the case of personality and in the specific case of the Big Four personality instrument, the ESTJ type (i.e. 'Thinking' not 'Feeling' types together with 'Sensing' and 'Judgement' types) is currently dominant in organisations, constituting 22% of types in an Ashridge study of type conducted with over 22,000 respondents (Carr et al., 2011), the largest single set of types in its dataset. The four personality predispositions that together feed into the ESTJ type create a tendency to make judgments and establish rules of behaviour to which others are expected to conform. As a consequence, the current tendency in organisations to recruit people with an ESTJ predisposition is likely to place psychological constraints on the creation of a more diverse and, to that extent, more divergent workforce. Given this fact, changing an organisation with a high proportion of ESTJ types is not likely to be easy. It might involve a highly concerted attempt at educating existing staff in the value of new ways of seeing, much as had been achieved in the public-sector probation services organisation that recognised the importance of a new style of leadership and adjusted its human resources procedures to ensure the presence of a more inclusive style of leader (Moss et al., 2006). However, doing this requires a high level of innovation on the part of the organisation and this may be hard to achieve in an organisation with a high proportion of ESTJ managers, something that may encourage the status quo recruitment seen in some organisations (Windolf, 1986).

The negative effect of status quo recruitment is linked to the fact that it can be 'conservative, often recruiting from the same social strata and age groups' of existing staff and can lead to organisational 'failure or at the very least stunted growth' (Boxall and Purcell, 2003, p. 140). The move to innovative recruitment and the search for a more heterogeneous group of applicants can help overcome these problems but this demands a shift in culture to ensure that prevailing values will not obstruct an appreciation of the output of people whose values and ways of seeing may be at odds with those of the conservative majority while being in line with those of the customer. We will discuss the implications of this later, meanwhile looking briefly at the alternative to innovative recruitment, namely training.

Given the context we are discussing here – namely the importation of customer-centric values to an organisation configured with a different set of values – training would need to educate existing incumbents about the alternative values of the customer. Doing this would include conveying information on the many and various 'ways of seeing' that exist and inculcating a methodology that involves shaping design and marketing solutions around the specific visual and thematic preferences of the target demographic. It has to be said, however, that even if people gain a logical understanding of the variety in people's preferences, people may still be limited in the extent to which they can think their way into another set of preferences. A further difficulty relates of course to the difficulty of identifying the personality types of the target market in the absence of the analytical possibilities available online when the language of those contributing to chat rooms can be analysed in terms of personality type, as described in Chapter 7, by Holly Buchanan.

We will now return to the issue of changing cultures, the step that paves the way for innovative recruitment, an option which offers a better long-term solution than training can ever do. A consideration of the issues involved in this is the focus of the next section.

Creating a culture that encourages diversity

While training people in a different way of seeing can be problematic, recruiting a diverse range of people who can mirror the thinking of the external customer can also be problematic until the internal culture is accepting of this difference. To develop a culture that is accepting of difference requires an inclusive style of leadership that will embrace and foster difference and not reject values, behaviours and people that are at odds with certain norms. We will therefore end this overview of personality within and outside organisations by considering the nature of inclusive leadership which could be a key element in allowing a shift in personality types to prevail in organisations.

According to one academic (Echols, 2009) and an empirical piece of research that the current author led (Moss et al., 2016; Moss, 2016), the competences needed for the delivery of the inclusive leadership style consist of the twin elements of transformational and servant leadership (Greenleaf, 1977), with 15 competencies associated with these collectively. These competencies draw on a number of interpersonal competencies (empathy, listening, healing, individualised attention) as well as broader cognitive competencies (foresight, conceptualising, awareness). A key question for organisations envisaging a shift from command and control to inclusive leadership relates to the personality features that are most likely to support the delivery of the interpersonal set of competencies described here.

Two personality instruments are the focus of previous studies, namely the Big Five (neuroticism, extraversion, openness to experience, agreeableness and conscientiousness) and the Big Four (extraversion/introversion, sensing/intuition, thinking/feeling and judgement/perception). Of the Big Five elements, one could imagine that those that would assist with the delivery of inclusive leadership could be the 'warmth' element of extraversion as well as agreeableness; of the Big Four elements, one could conceive that the 'feeling' element would make an important contribution.

Unfortunately, recent research is at best divided or at worst negative on one or more of these elements. So, where 'agreeableness' is concerned for example one study (Howard and Bray, 1988) found it to be negatively correlated with managerial potential, another two studies (Judge and Bono, 2000; Srivastava, 2011) found it to be positively correlated with overall job performance and managerial effectiveness, while a third study (Moutafi et al., 2007) found no relationship with managerial level. The difference in these findings is potentially confusing until it is realised that different notions of managerial effectiveness could be assumed in different studies since assumptions about the style of management presumed (e.g. whether transactional or transformational) are not spelt out. This lack of clarity regarding managerial assumptions may explain why the 'warmth' element of extraversion (part of the 'Big Five') is not correlated with managerial seniority (Moutafi et al., 2007) and why the 'feeling' element of the Big Four is associated only with an enhancement in innovation (Moutafi et al., 2007). If a transactional model is assumed, a style heavily reliant on command and control, one could understand why warmth and feeling might not be at a premium, while a presumption of transformational leadership, an integral element of inclusive leadership, might make this lack of correlation less easy to understand.

Key role of leadership

To achieve an inclusive form of leadership will help organisations to embrace diversity with greater ease and help ensure that an outside-inside perspective gains ground in organisations. A major focus needs to be devoted to this since, as many commentators have told us, leadership has the potential to change organisations dramatically. As an instance of this, Ken Blanchard, visiting professor at Cornell University, has indicated that leaders have a major role in setting the vision that inspires movement towards an organisation's goals to move towards the organisation's goals, and then creating a motivating environment that assists people in reaching these goals. As he says, excellent leaders can turn a good organisation into a great one, and poor leaders can, in his view, 'send a great organisation downhill' (Blanchard, 2011).

A more efficient organisation is one that is responsive to its customer base and the leadership style and culture will be key elements in ensuring that customer needs can be met. An inclusive leadership style will help achieve this and will also produce other benefits not possible with its opposite, the command and control style. These include bringing subgroups together and ensuring cognitive diversity, something that the emerging millennial generation (born 1980–1995), now 35% of the UK workforce, is more likely than earlier generations to view as essential for an organisational culture (Deloitte, 2015; Smith, 2015). What is more, the greater volatility, uncertainty, complexity and ambiguity (VUCA) in the environments (Wolf, 2007) are more easily managed through inclusive leadership than the more inflexible command and control style (Fiedler, 1958).

So, many prizes await the organisation that has a more inclusive style of leadership, not least of which is the ability of the organisation to match internal personality types with those of the customer. Once that has been done, the ability to understand the customer and thereby meet the customer's needs will be all the greater.

References

Alimo-Metcalfe, B. and Alban-Metcalfe, J. (2005). Leadership: Time for a new direction? *Leadership*, 1, February, pp. 51–71, accessed on 18 October 2015 at http://www.ctrtraining.co.uk/documents/AlimoMetcalfeLeadershipTimeforaNewDirection.pdf.

Baden-Fuller, C. (1995). Strategic innovation, corporate entrepreneurship and matching outside-in to inside-out approaches to strategy research. *British Journal of Management*, 6(s1), pp. s3–s16.

Balogun, J. and Hope Hailey, V. (2008) *Exploring Strategic Change*, 3rd edition. Harlow: Prentice Hall.

Bass, B. (1998). *Transformational Leadership: Industrial, Military, and Educational Impact.* Mahwah, NJ: Lawrence Erlbaum.

Blanchard, K. (2011). Why does leadership matter, 8 October, available at http://howwelead.org/2011/10/08/why-does-leadership-matter/, accessed on 18 December 2015.

Boxall, P. and Purcell, J. (2003). *Strategy and Human Resource Management.* Basingstoke: Palgrave Macmillan.

Brock, T. C. (1965). Communicator-recipient similarity and decision change. *Journal of Personality and Social Psychology*, 1, pp. 650–54.

Byrne, D. and Neuman, J. (1992). The implications of attraction research for organizational issues, in Kelley, K. (ed.) *Issues, Theory and Research in Industrial and Organizational Psychology*. New York: Elsevier.

Carr, M., Curd, J., Davda, F. and Piper, N. (2011). MBTI research into distribution of type, Ashridge Business School, available at https://www.ashridge.org.uk/Media-Library/Ashridge/PDFs/Publications/MBTIResearchIntoDistribution2.pdf, accessed on 9 April 2016.

Catalyst (2014). Inclusive leadership: The view from six countries, available at http://www.catalyst.org/system/files/inclusive_leadership_the_view_from_six_countries_0.pdf, accessed on 1 October 2015.

Centre for Applications of Psychological Type. (n.d.). Estimated frequencies of the types in the United States population. https://www.capt.org/mbti-assessment/estimated-frequencies.htm, accessed on 12 October 2016.

Chernatony, L. de and Drury, S. (2004). Identifying and sustaining services brands values. *Journal of Marketing Communications*, 10, pp. 73–94.

Crozier, W. R. and Greenhalgh, P. (1992). The empathy principle: Towards a model for the psychology of art. *Journal for the Theory of Social Behaviour*, 22(1), pp. 63–79.

Davies, E. (2013). Women on boards, available at https://www.gov.uk/government/uploads/system/uploads/attachment_data/file/182602/bis-13-p135-women-on-boards-2013.pdf, accessed on 9 April 2016.

Deloitte (2015). Fourth millennial survey: Mind the gaps, available at http://www2.deloitte.com/global/en/pages/about-deloitte/articles/millennialsurvey.html, accessed on 26 October 2015.

Dipboye, R. and Macan, T. (1988). A process view of the selection/recruitment interview, in Schuler, R., Youngblood, S. and Huber, V. (eds.), *Readings in Personnel and Human Resource Management*. St Paul, MN: West.

Donovan, R. J., Rossiter, J. R., Marcoolyn, G. and Nesdale, A. (1994). Store atmosphere and purchasing behaviour. *Journal of Retailing*, 70(3), pp. 283–294.

Driscoll, Dawn-Marie and Hoffman, W. Michael. (2000). *Ethics Matters: How to Implement Values-Driven Management*. Waltham, MA: Bently College Center for Business Ethics.

Echols, S. (2009). Transformational/servant leadership: A potential synergism for an inclusive leadership style. *Journal of Religious Leadership*, 8(2), pp. 85–116, available at http://arl-jrl.org/Volumes/Echols09.pdf, accessed on 8 July 2015.

Fiedler, F. E. (1958). *Leader Attitudes and Group Effectiveness*. Urbana: University of Illinois Press.

Greenleaf, R. K. (1977). *Servant Leadership: A Journey into the Nature of Legitimate Power and Greatness*. New York: Paulist Press.

Groppel, A. (1993). Store design and experience orientated consumers in retailing: Comparison between the United States and Germany, in Van Raaij, W. F. and Bassomy, G. J. (eds.), *European Advances in Consumer Research*. Amsterdam: Association for Consumer Research.

Hammer, E. F. (1980). *The Clinical Application of Projective Drawings*. Springfield: Charles C. Thomas.

Hammer, M. (1995). *Reengineering the Corporation*. London: Nicholas Brealey.

Howard, A. and Bray, D. W. (1988). *Management Lives in Transition: Advancing Age and Changing Times*. New York: Guilford Press.

International Labour Organization (ILO). (2015). Women in business and management: Gaining momentum, available at http://www.ilo.org/wcmsp5/groups/public/—-dgreports/—-dcomm/—-publ/documents/publication/wcms_334882.pdf, accessed on 30 September.

Janz, B. D., and Prasarnphanich, P. (2003), Understanding the antecedents of effective knowledge management: The importance of a knowledge-centered culture. *Decision Sciences*, 34(2), pp. 351–384.

Judge, T. A. and Bono, J. E. (2000). Personality and job satisfaction: The mediating role of job characteristics. *Journal of Applied Psychology*, 85, pp. 237–249.

Karande, K., Zinkhan, G. M. and Lum, A. B. (1997). Brand personality and self concept: A replication and extension. *American Marketing Association, Summer Conference*, 8, pp. 165–171.

Lewis, C. (2006). Is the test relevant? *Times*, 30 November, p. 8.

Moss, G. (2007). The impact of personality and gender on branding decisions. *Journal of Brand Management*, 14(4), pp. 277–283.

Moss, G. (2009). *Gender, Design and Marketing: How Gender Drives Our Perception of Design and Marketing*. Farnham: Gower.

Moss, G. (2014). Unconscious bias as a mechanism for indirect discrimination. *Equal Opportunities Review*, 252, November, pp. 11–12.

Moss, G. (2016). Inclusive leadership: Boosting engagement, productivity and organisational diversity. *Equal Opportunities Review*, June, pp. 5–8.

Moss, G. and Daunton, L. (2006). The discriminatory impact of deviations from selection criteria in higher education selection. *Career Development International* 11(6), pp. 504–21.

Moss, G., Daunton, L. and Gasper. (2006). The impact of leadership selection on high performance working. *CIPD Professional Standards Conference*, 26–28 June 2006, Keele University.

Moss, G., Gunn, R. and Kubacki, K. (2008). Gender and web design: The implications of the mirroring principle for the services branding model. *Journal of Marketing Communications*, 14(1), pp. 37–57.

Moss, G., Sims, C., Dodds, I. and David, A. (2016). Inclusive leadership . . . driving performance through diversity. Employers Network on Equality and Inclusion, available at http://www.enei.org.uk/pages/inclusive-leadership-...-driving-performance-through-diversity.html

Moutafi, J., Furnham, A. and Crump, J. (2007). Is managerial level related to personality? *British Journal of Management*, 1, pp. 272–280.

Page, R., Jagger, N., Tamkin, P. and Henwood, N. (2006). The measurement of organisational performance. *Institute of Employment Studies*, available at http://www.employment-studies.co.uk/resource/measurement-organisational-performance, accessed on 23 April 2016.

Porteous, J. D. (1996). *Environmental Aesthetics: Ideas, Politics and Planning*. London: Routledge.

Russell, R. and Stone, A. (2002). A review of servant leadership attributes: Developing a practical model. *Leadership and Organisation Development Journal*, 23(3), pp. 145–157.

Schneider, R. (2001). Variety performance. *People Management*, 7(9), pp. 27–31.

Smith, C. (2015). The radical transformation of diversity and inclusion the millennial influence, Deloitte University, available at http://www2.deloitte.com/us/en/pages/about-deloitte/articles/radical-transformation-of-diversity-and-inclusion.html, accessed on 25 August 2015.

Srivastava, S. (2011). Assessing the relationship between personality variable and managerial effectiveness: An empirical study on private sector managers. *Management and Labour Studies*, 36(4), pp. 319–333.

Windolf, P. (1986). Recruitment, selection and internal labour markets in Britain and Germany. *Organisational Studies*, 7(3), pp. 235–254.

Wolf, Daniel. (2007). *Prepared and Resolved: The Strategic Agenda for Growth, Performance and Change*. Grand Rapids, MI: dsb Publishing.

Yahomoto, M. and Lambert, D. R. (1994). The impact of product aesthetics on the evaluation of industrial products. *Journal of Product Innovation Management*, 11, pp. 309–324.

Index